JOB Unlocked – A Revelation
By Randy Winters

www.jobunlocked.com

All rights reserved. Written permission must be secured from the publisher to use or reproduce any part of this book, except for brief quotations in critical reviews or articles.

Published in Carlsbad, California by Randy Winters

Unless otherwise noted, Scripture quotations are from the NIV Study Bible New International Version by Zondervan Publishing House. Copyright 1985. All rights reserved.

ISBN: 978-0-9910611-0-5

© 2013 by Randy Winters

In dedication to:
God
Jesus
Holy Spirit

Inspiration:

Deana Winters - My wife
Brigette Winters – Daughter
Nathan Winters - Son
Jon Eldridge - Author
Todd Spath - Family Therapist and Evangelist
Dani Johnson - Business Trainer
Kip McKean - Evangelist
Kevin Holland – Evangelist
David Graham - Musician
Carlos Mejia – Evangelist
Jeff Morrell – Friend
Kai and BJ Foster - Evangelists
The Family of God

Contents

INTRODUCTION 4
CATACLYSMIC EVENTS 6
A DISTURBING DREAM 19
THE UNSEEN FIGURE 34
BREAK THE MAN 50
GOD'S LAWS 60
THE CHARACTER WEAPON 77
TWISTER 90
DYING BEFORE DENYING 102
WET SANDWICH 115
FREEDOM OF CHOICE 127
THE LOVE SYNDROME 139
NOT FORSAKEN 152
THE MOST RIGHTEOUS PERSON 162
THE RICH YOUNG RULER 174
THE CALL 183

Introduction

If God did not exist, what would be the purpose of doing good, treating people right, or believing in love or righteousness? Any attempt at living life without love and righteousness would be pointless. If at the end of life you go into oblivion and cease to exist, then all you did while living becomes worthless, useless, futile, and without meaning. However, if God exists, then we have a responsibility to know who God is and what is expected from our lives. Through our knowledge of God, we then realize he is more than we can ever imagine. He lives beyond our imaginations. He affects life even to the core of our soul, mind, and spirit. Amazing capabilities he has.

I have been studying the Bible for over 20 years and am astonished at the depth of knowledge contained in the scriptures. I have watched miracles right before my eyes that were difficult to absorb and accept. I watched the crash and burn of individuals who were at one time examples in the faith to see them stand right back up to go at it again. I watched people struggle to understand the words contained in the Bible and come out with an understanding.

Certain scriptures, books, concepts, and words in the Bible are difficult to understand. JOB is such a book. Most commentaries or sermons on JOB would leave me agitated for some reason. Being agitated made me realize there must be something missing, something important. However, I accepted the teaching, but in the back of my mind lay an unanswered question of agitation.

The book of JOB has not been understood for centuries. The journey you will take through this book will answer some questions, but open more questions. If God had informed Job before going through his ordeal about what he was going to endure, we would have a completely different story. We would have a story with little meaning or affect. We would not have the wealth of knowledge contained in the story. Opening the doorway to a new understanding is always welcomed and this is it.

In South Africa, a philosophy known as UBUNTU says, *"the only way for me to be human is for you to reflect my humanity back at me."* It also says, "There is no way for us to be human without other people." The hope is that this book will reflect humanity back to the reader to gain a new understanding, not only about the Bible, but their life, and the lives that surround them.

If you have not read the book of JOB for quite some time, or have not read it at all, I encourage you to read it along side reading this book for the benefit of a deeper understanding.

Cataclysmic Events

Ahhhh……..JOB. The most confusing, misunderstood, questionable, misinterpreted, soul twisting, mind-bending book ever to be written. Everyone I have ever talked to has the same unnerving feeling inside after having read the book. It is the combination of the thought of all the cataclysmic events that took place in JOB's life and God's response to JOB after allowing JOB to go through what he did. God's response pushes buttons inside all of us causing a wide range of emotions. Even the fact that we know God put it in the Bible for a reason does not make it any easier to accept. Hopefully, after this journey, the confusion will be lifted.

A classic example of this type of confusion can be seen in the show Just For Laughs. A group of people I will call "gagsters" set up a situation that causes people to laugh, be confused, or think twice about what just happened. I will give you an example. Three people in on a gag are placed in a store. A police officer enters later.

The cashier, in on the gag, accidentally leaves a wad of cash on the counter for some unknown reason and walks away. Gagster (1) looks at the cash, grabs it, and runs out the door as the gag victim steps to the counter to pay. Gagster (2) looks at the victim with a "what just happened" look. The cashier comes back as a police officer walks in and the cashier reports the situation.

The police officer runs out, catches gagster (1), and brings him back. The gag victim says he saw gagster (1) take the money. Gagster (1) denies the allegation and says gagster (2) took the money. The cashier rewinds a phony video tape from the time of the theft and shows gagster (2), not (1), taking the money. The police officer reaches into the pocket of gagster (2) and finds the money. The victim is overcome with confusion because they saw gagster (1) take the money. Thinking about JOB gives me a similar "is you kidding me????" feeling.

Let us have a short recap of JOB for a moment. Here is a man, who God believes no other man is similar in his love, respect, devotion, loyalty, heart, etc., etc., just walking along doing his daily activities and all of a sudden, wham, disaster wipes out his family, servants, animals, and livelihood. JOB tears his robe and takes the time to shave his head. Tearing your clothes is a form of expressing righteous indignation or grief and shaving your head is a sign of mourning.

All I can say is "WHAT?" Here is a man who there is no other man like him and God allows him to be destroyed. *"But spare his life,"* God says. So, if I follow God, "I am not assured a good life" is the message. If I get it right then, I have a life where one moment I could be having a great time and in the next moment, I could be despairing for my very existence. Sounds like how I felt when the one I loved in high school did not want to start naming our children and practicing to change diapers…with me at least.

If that was not enough, at some point later, JOB receives boils on his skin while being "blameless and upright and maintaining integrity." JOB's wife comes in and tells him to stop maintaining integrity, curse God, and die. She must have been really mad herself because of the loss of all her servants, Versace clothes, Christian Dior shoes, Yves Saint Laurent perfume -- you get the point. JOB was wealthy and could afford the very best for his wife. She basically says, "Why don't you die because you are no good for me now." I am sure she knew the laws of God and thought he had committed an unfathomable sin. Of all the disaster that took place in JOB's life, this one was probably the hardest to take at that point of his destruction. A non-compassionate and non-loving wife during an extremely difficult time in a man's life is challenging to say the least.

However, I do not know what his wife was going through at that time. Her grief could have caused her to say those irrational things to her husband, but I do not know.

I have been very lucky to have a wife that supports me during the times I have been in rough situations. The support of my wife gave me the strength to make it through those situations and come out the other side still in the battle and loving God.

JOB remained righteous and was right about his situation, but God won the argument. Just like a married man and woman; the man may be right about the situation, but the woman wins the argument. Well, not all the time. Anyway...

I just love the way God enters my life at times. While writing this chapter, God peaked into my life and said, "Hi, I have something for you." I have been going through the Biblegateway 'Read the Bible in a Year' program and on the day I was writing about JOB's wife, the chapter sent to me from Biblegateway was Leviticus 24 which coincides with what I was writing about that day.

Leviticus 24:13-16 says, "Then the LORD said to Moses: *"Take the blasphemer outside the camp. All those who heard him are to lay their hands on his head, and the entire assembly is to stone him. Say to the Israelites: 'Anyone who curses their God will be held responsible; anyone who blasphemes the name of the LORD is to be put to death. The entire assembly must stone them. Whether foreigner or native-born, when they blaspheme the Name they are to be put to death."* JOB would have been put to death according to Law, if he cursed God. JOB's wife was saying he was better off dead than alive.

However, JOB does not curse God, but curses the day of his birth. He protests his situation, pleads for an explanation, and stops short of accusing God of injustice. Satan was sure JOB would curse God if God had removed his barrier of protection. Satan was wrong.

Now, JOB's friends show up and we get the idea they sat on the ground next to JOB for 7 days as a form of consoling and having compassion for JOB. However, there were laws about diseases and laws about what to do when a person has a disease.

In Leviticus 13, the specifics about boils say a person must be pronounced as ceremonially unclean because they are affected with a defiling skin disease. The priests are to isolate the affected person for seven days. In JOB 2:12 it says, *"When they saw him from a distance, they could hardly recognize him; they began to weep aloud, and they tore their robes and sprinkled dust on their heads. [13] Then they sat on the ground with him for seven days and seven nights."* JOB's friends sat on the ground at a distance because JOB was in isolation. They did not say a word because they would have had to talk very loud or scream in order to talk to JOB. They knew he was suffering and therefore did not say a word hoping that in 7 days his suffering would subside and being able to get closer to him, could talk to him then.

Who were JOB's friends? There were a total of four. We know three were older than JOB by the comment in JOB 15:9-10 *"What insights do you have that we do not have? The gray-haired and the aged are on our side."* The older friends expected JOB to have respect for his elders because of their wisdom of years. One was younger, which was Elihu, the last one to respond.

The men set out after hearing about JOB *"to go and sympathize with him and comfort him."* This one statement has been used as the drive or catalyst to summarize all of the conversations held between JOB and his friends and describes what they were trying to achieve in their conversations. In my mind, I did not agree with that interpretation because it never made sense to me, but I could not figure out why. Therefore, I accepted this concept, as did everyone else. This book holds the key to a new view of why JOB was written.

God, at the end of the book, never tells JOB what happened nor gives any compassion and only challenges JOB with questions of whether or not he created every living thing, created the expanses in the sky, the dividing lines of air, water, mountains, and so on. God tells JOB's friends they have not spoken the truth. Eliphaz is instructed to take seven bulls and seven rams to JOB, as atonement for him and his friends, and JOB will pray for them and God will accept JOB's prayer. And finally, God gives back to JOB double what he had in the beginning.

Now, I do not know about you, but that does not appear to be just and fair in my mind, well, except for the very last part where JOB gets twice what he had in the beginning. Of course, fairness and justice in my mind looks like what I think it is. My idea of justice and fairness usually ensures I win in the process. Even though I desire to be just and fair, it is not possible all by myself without God.

Fairness in God's mind is much different. In The Parable of the Workers in the Vineyard, Matthew 20 is a good example in that the hired help work different amounts of time and receive the same pay. Matthew 25, The Parable of the Ten Virgins, all the virgins waited together and when it was time to go in to the wedding banquet, only the ones with oil were let in.

However, fairness is not part of the story of JOB. I believe it was not fair that JOB went through what he did. Why would God allow this to be done to his creation (people) when he loves them to the point of allowing his son to die on a cross for us? This makes no sense to me. I think of it in terms of why would I allow a truck to run over our child only to see that he survives. I love our children too much to ever allow them go through anything that horrific, especially if I can stop it.

The story of JOB defies logic, charges our emotional state toward inconceivable confusion, and leaves us with so much mental turmoil that we have to just let it go and accept we understand very little of the story.

To be fair to the concept of compassion, I would like to travel down the path that JOB's friends were actually trying to be compassionate toward JOB. I looked for statements of love, enduring friendship, peace, patience, kindness, or goodness. Here are some statements that stood out as I perused my way through the conversations.

These verses are supposed to reflect compassion and comfort:

JOB 4:7 Consider now: Who, being innocent, has ever perished?
JOB, you are not innocent. You are guilty.

JOB 4:8 As I have observed, those who plow evil.
JOB, you have plowed evil.

JOB 8:13 Such is the destiny of all who forget God; so perishes the hope of the godless.
Meaning: JOB, you are godless.

JOB 11:3 Will your idle talk reduce others to silence? Will no one rebuke you when you mock?
JOB, you are mocking God.

JOB 11:12 But the witless can no more become wise than a wild donkey's colt can be born human.
JOB, you are Witless and stupid.

JOB 11:20 But the eyes of the wicked will fail, and escape will elude them; their hope will become a dying gasp."
JOB, you are wicked.

JOB 15:2 Would a wise person answer with empty notions or fill their belly with the hot east wind?
JOB, you are stupid and have no intelligent words.

JOB 15:5 Your sin prompts your mouth; you adopt the tongue of the crafty.
JOB, you are crafty and sly creating words to your benefit.

JOB 18:5 The lamp of a wicked man is snuffed out; the flame of his fire stops burning.
JOB, you are a wicked man to think as he does.

JOB 18:12 It eats away parts of his skin; death's firstborn devours his limbs.
Such a loving compassionate statement for someone in such pain.

JOB 20:6 & 7 Though the pride of the godless person reaches to the heavens and his head touches the clouds, he will perish forever, like his own dung.
JOB, you are so prideful that it reaches to the heavens to perish forever like dung.

JOB 22:4 Is it for your piety that he rebukes you and brings charges against you?
JOB, you are flattering yourself to the point of being equal to God.

JOB 22:15 Will you keep to the old path that the wicked have trod?

JOB, you are on the path of the wicked

JOB 34:11 He repays everyone for what they have done; he brings on them what their conduct deserves.
Even Elihu, who is younger than JOB, accuses him with this statement.

JOB 34:35 JOB speaks without knowledge; his words lack insight.
JOB, you are stupid and speak empty words.

JOB 35:12 He does not answer when people cry out because of the arrogance of the wicked.
JOB, you are arrogant and wicked.

Therefore, as I understand here, I am supposed to be speaking this kind of compassion to my family and friends on a daily basis. This is the epitome of compassion and consolation. I need to be addressing my wife in the same way. Of course, I am being sarcastic here. The conversation between JOB and his friends was not one of compassion or consoling. Their conversations were laden with attacks upon JOB. These attacks were targeting specific ideas and concepts. Why were they attacking JOB? What would prompt them to attack JOB instead of offer compassion and consolation? Were they out of their minds?

I realize I am not at all different from JOB's friends when I experience people who are afflicted in some way. Some afflictions are physically evident and others are not. Compassion cannot be easily expressed by most of us. People with visible disabilities in wheelchairs are a good example of this. My heart goes out to them. On the other hand, I have a difficult time expressing my compassion to people with inward afflictions such as depression. JOB's friends had visible evidence and they still chose not to be compassionate.

JOB is the personification and an example of what we are going through – affliction. We are to be un-afflicted some day in heaven, but right now, we are all afflicted in some way groaning under the pressure. Even on the day I write this, my wife and I were praying and groaning about the situation we have been in for such a long time. I wish I could say we had a financial situation, but we do not have enough finances to call it a situation. God has still taken care of our needs over the years. We are not unique in our affliction. JOB made it through. If we make it, we inherit a kingdom. All the while, we are frustrated in our affliction because we desire to be in heaven enjoying peace forever.

Affliction is the testing of our hearts to see if we are truly steadfast in God. In the moments of our affliction, do we still see God there for us? There was a time when I was deeply afflicted and hurt by my wife. As I lay in the grass at a park pondering my predicament, I got up to use the park restroom.

Walking to the restroom, I realized a homeless person walking straight toward me and looking at me with piercing eyes. It was as if he reached in and touched my soul with his eyes. I turned to go into the restroom and later made it back to my spot in the park where I had been laying in anger.

The homeless person decided to lie down and rest under a tree not far from where I was. I could not help thinking about the contact between the homeless person and myself. And, for some reason, "forgiveness" came to mind. I thought many homeless people needed either to be forgiven or to forgive someone. Then it dawned on me. I need to forgive my wife. Ouch! I also needed to ask for forgiveness from my wife too.

As I lay with my head on the grass, I struggled with the thought and eventually forgave her. I looked up to find the homeless person so I could go over and thank him for what he caused in my heart, but he was nowhere to be found. I had just looked at him not more than 30 seconds to a minute before. I was in awe at the amazing event that just took place. I thought about Jesus on the cross and the words he chose to say. He could have said a multitude of words, but he spoke the most powerful words anyone can speak and acknowledge, "forgiveness."

Like JOB, I wanted justification. Like JOB, I wanted God to come and pat me on the back saying what a good servant I was; to tell me not to worry about the conflict between my wife and me because I was in the right. It did not matter who was right or wrong though, because she is my wife. It did not matter who was right or wrong because that is God. If I love my wife, I will forgive and move on. If I love my God, I will forgive and move on. JOB could have forgiven God because there was no sin, but JOB wanted to be right and justified just as I did.

Life has many difficulties whether financially, physically, spiritually, or other, and surviving through those ups and downs while rejoicing as 1 Peter 1:6 says is not something we think about when we go through suffering or hard times. 1 Peter 1:6 *"In all this you greatly rejoice, though now for a little while you may have had to suffer grief in all kinds of trials."* JOB had his trials all at once it seems. Through his trial, JOB did not sin by charging God with wrongdoing. I find it incredibly amazing that JOB did not charge God with wrongdoing. That just tells me I am nothing like JOB. I have not found anyone on the planet so far that has not had "accusations" in their heart for something whether it is a person, place, or thing. How could JOB refuse those accusations toward God? Where did he get the strength and conviction, especially when JOB knew he was right?

I cannot say the same thing. I have mounted piles of evidence to charge God with wrongdoing. I have told God he made wrong decisions about my life. As a young Christian, I stood on a mountaintop angrily yelling at God because certain things did not come to fruition in my life I had been praying for. On that occasion, he answered me immediately, which was awesome, but not so awesome too. I turned around to see 100 yards down the hill a police officer giving me ticket for illegally parking. I was humbled. I still plead my case with God every now and then, but without anger. Although, I am changing and have come to the realization that God knows better than I do.

My wife and I met and lived in Los Angeles. We moved near San Diego to start a new life with our newly adopted children. The last seven years have been challenging but incredibly full of learning, growing, and changing. We started a business that failed miserably and had to redirect our lives rather quickly. I could not find work and went back to college to get a degree while my wife worked. I had to do the Mr. Mom gig along with class studies. Little did I know how God had reached into my heart and pulled out a deep desire of mine to get a degree I did not even know was there. I am learning that God knows me better than I do and to trust his decisions. Trusting his decisions is not so simple and easy. Nothing is simple and easy in life.

The book of JOB is broken down into two chapters of devastation, 36 chapters of conversation between JOB and friends, and 5 chapters of conversation between JOB and God. I believe that if God had wanted the devastating acts to be important, He would have expanded the chapters a lot more. I tend to think the two chapters of devastation are not that important.

Something more important is at stake within the 36 chapters of conversation between JOB and his friends. This is a lot of talking between friends that has been carefully written down for us. What is the importance of those chapters? Why has God given us 36 chapters of conversation and we focus on the two chapters of devastation. Is there something else that God wants to tell us? Why is it that when I look at those compassionate statements, I do not believe they were meant to be compassionate.

We always focus on the two chapters where JOB experiences devastating circumstances allowed by God. These are important chapters; however, because they lead the way to understanding what JOB had remaining in his life after the devastation. JOB lost everything. What did he have left? He had no house, children, servants, animals, his wife mentally left him, his health left him, and he was driven down to the point where it was just between him and God. JOB had nothing left but his beliefs, which I believe Satan targeted using JOB's friends.

If all JOB had was his belief of who God was and what God stood for, then breaking this belief is the real target of the story. How does one destroy or change beliefs? This is a good question.

One of the most devastating stories of someone who damaged people's beliefs is Jim Jones. Jim Jones, the founder of the Peoples Temple, in 1978 coerced 914 people to commit suicide. Jim's mother believed she had given birth to a messiah. Jim Jones had some disturbed ideas while leading people under the premise of religion. Those people were fooled into committing suicide through a destructive belief pattern.

As Christians, we need to be on the alert. Individuals claiming to have the special anointing to give God's word to the masses can fool us to acquiring certain beliefs. This is why it is so important for everyone who wants to know God to study the Bible and compare notes with those around them. Your pastor will not get you to heaven. YOU will get yourself to heaven. Your pastor can only help you make the right choices.

As for JOB, we will explore the idea that the first two chapters were important, but the other 36 contain more value. These are the chapters God wants us to understand because the first two chapters open the door to the other 36.

A Disturbing Dream

The light from the afternoon sun flooded through the room window. For some reason I stood in a corner looking into the middle of the room. I had this overwhelming urge to flap my arms up and down. This feeling of being able to fly came over me telling me to move my arms faster and faster. As I felt the wind from my arms, to my surprise I lifted off the ground. This was utter ecstasy to feel the impossible.

I came back down to the ground and quickly ran outside to see how far I could get up into the air. I was flying. As I swooped down over people standing around, I kept telling them that all they had to do is flap their arms. Some could do it, but some were not able to feel the excitement of flying. The adrenaline of flying finally subsided, and I came back to the ground. I stood there smiling over what had just happened. The amazement raced through my veins and suddenly I awoke from my dream. I was both ecstatic and saddened that the experience had ended.

I dream a lot while sleeping, or even awake. In my awakened state, I create scenarios or relive past experiences changing the outcomes to fit my expectations. The variety of dreams I have had over a lifetime cannot be counted. Some of the dreams have been about volcanoes erupting near my hotel room, only being able to open my eyes lids with my fingers, not being able to run because some force is against me preventing me from moving quickly, chewing a large amount of gum that sticks in my mouth and finding it difficult to get it out, and only one time in my life do I remember dreaming while in a dream.

Dreaming while dreaming was strange. I awoke from a dream only to find I was still dreaming. The second level of the dream was in black and white and quite odd in a death sort of way. I believe dreaming is quite universal and useful for a variety of issues in our life. Dream interpreters describe the meaning of dreams in an effort to help people understand dreams.

Where do dreams come from? Why are dreams important? What are the meanings of dreams? How do they affect us in our lives? We all have these questions about dreams and some seek out advisors of dreams.

Dreams are described as a succession of images, thoughts, or emotions passing through the mind during sleep as well as an involuntary or voluntary vision occurring to a person when awake. A dream can also be a goal. Dreams can be prophetic, contain wisdom, crazy, nonsensical, and nightmarish containing never before or already experienced people, places, and things.

Interpreting dreams is elusive. One person says one thing and another person says something different. Sometimes they are close in meaning with slight differences. There are a lot of "could be's" within dream interpretation. The dream 'could' mean this, or the dream 'could' mean that, and have no relation to each other. For instance, dreaming of seeing or eating celery is supposed to represent your need to be cleansed either physically or emotionally, but it 'could' be an indication of your financial concerns; being a pun on "salary."

Dreaming about celebrities means to be good friends with a celebrity, which represents your idealized version of someone you know in your life. You 'could' be hoping that a real-life friend would act more like a particular celebrity. You need to examine the qualities you see in the celebrity and how you want your friends to have those qualities. However, it 'could' also mean you are trying to compensate for your own lack of self-confidence. You desire to escape from your reality and live a life of extravagance. On the other hand, you 'could' just want to fit in.

The interpretation of anger in your dreams by either holding or expressing your anger symbolizes frustrations and disappointments in yourself. You tend to repress your negative emotions or project your anger onto others. The solution is to look inside you. Fortunately, I do not have dreams of anger because I let it out on unwilling receivers of my wrath. I have tried to bottle it up and gain control, but this is an issue God has been working with me for a long time. I have gotten better, but I still need work in this area.

Information in dreams can only come from three sources. First, we see in the Bible that God gives us information in dreams to further his quest for our redemption. We know we, ourselves, are the source of information in dreams. Finally, yet most importantly, Satan can deliver and affect our dreams. I will not go into this right now, but you will see the evidence later.

Let us examine the process of God providing information for our dreams and how they are delivered and interpreted. In the book of Daniel, chapter two, King Nebuchadnezzar had a dream and he wanted his astrologers to tell him what he dreamed and what it meant. He told them he was going to destroy them and their houses if they did not interpret the dream.

God purposely gave Nebuchadnezzar a dream as well as urged him not to divulge his dream to his astrologers so that Daniel, the one and only holy man in the land, could tell him what it was and what it meant.

Daniel pleaded with God and the meaning of the dream was revealed in a vision. Daniel was not only able to tell Nebuchadnezzar what he dreamed but what it meant as well.

The dream was used to express to Nebuchadnezzar the coming destruction, but more importantly was the catalyst to the change of heart by Nebuchadnezzar to admit that the God of Daniel was the lord of lords. Nebuchadnezzar was a tough cookie to break, so God had to give more dreams, have

Shadrach, Meshach and Abednego walk in a furnace, remove him from his kingdom and finally, Nebuchadnezzar repented.

I have had some prophetic dreams given to me by God. At first, it was difficult to believe my prophetic dreams and visions had value to anyone because I had no proof that what I was experiencing was something real. I had some dreams I thereafter expressed to certain individuals. The messages of the dreams I expressed to those individuals had meaning, importance, and provided proof for me because of what was reported to me afterward.

The first of these types of dreams were simple. I had felt something was not quite right with a certain 16-year-old female teen within our church. My heart was moved, but I could not understand why. I was not close to the family but only knew of them from a distance.

One night I was told in a dream to communicate with the teen's father a message I believed was from God. I was completely anxious and afraid to express the information because I had no proof it was from God, but proceeded to do so. The message was that the father was responsible for something. I did not know what it was; just that he was responsible for something about his daughter. He was receptive but perplexed about this vague message.

Three weeks later, the man's wife I had spoken to contacted my wife to express that what I had dreamed was correct and the depth of the situation was more than the family could fathom. The dream had prepared the family for what was exposed.

Having a communicated dream come true was twofold for me. I was devastated because of the problem that was exposed. At the same time, I was honored and humbled that God would use me to open up this hidden topic within the family. So, needless to say, I now pay attention to dreams more closely.

The possibility that dreams could affect my life as well as others became very real for me and is the reason for authoring this book. I have had other dreams directly affecting individuals I gave the message to as well. I have also given messages to individuals I have no way of knowing whether the message meant anything in their life.

The next dream I will explain is the catalyst for me writing and exposing the very essence of the meaning on the book of JOB. The dream opened my mind to understand and perceive JOB on a completely different level than I had learned through the acceptance of the basic theory of compassion by JOB's friends. The confusion lifted as I contemplated what was exposed. I was compelled to expose the message.

The dream given to me by God was one of the most intense I have ever experienced. Initially, the dream had meaning for a friend of mine, but through that meaning, came the doorway to reinterpret the story of JOB.

In the dream, I was standing outside in the dimly lit darkness with two other friends. Both of these friends I knew very well, however, one of my friends had stopped reading the Bible, going to church, and was getting a divorce. My friend had been losing his faith for quite awhile through events between him and his wife. His faith and belief about God was dissipating like the morning dew on a sunny day. The other friend goes to church and has sons who read the Bible and try to live their life as Jesus did.

The three of us were standing outside in the dark and suddenly something flew down, opened its mouth, and swallowed, from head to toe, my friend who had stopped reading the Bible. Upon seeing this event that just happened, I realized the figure was a demon.

My idea of a demon is probably not the same as other people. When I envision a demon, I see a thin frail human body with thin bat wings about 10 feet in width riddled with veins. They have two horns on their heads about two or three inches in length. Their eyes were red which made them more seeable in the darkness. Their skin looked like smooth leather with a pale gray-beige color. Their mouths were cable of opening the width of a human body.

When they swallowed my friend, it was as if he only swallowed his spirit because the demon's body did not expand as if swallowing a physical body. My guess was that we did not have physical bodies in the dream, just spiritual. The demons would stay in the trees and then swoop down upon the humans walking around on the ground.

I turned to my other friend that was with me and told him to look up into the air so that when a demon flew down, we would be able to see the demon and possibly prevent the demon from swallowing us. He told me he was afraid of looking up at the demons. Seeing the demons caused great fear in his soul. I tried to coerce him look at the demons but he would not look. Just then, a demon swooped down over the top of my head and I woke up from the dream.

As I lay there in my bed, I realized the reason the demon ate up one of my friends. His beliefs about God had literally vanished from his soul. He became vulnerable to the attack from losing his beliefs. At one point in my friend's life, he had believed in God's promises and lived a life imitating Jesus. Slowly, over time, my friend had lost interest in understanding God and living according to God's principles. Initially, he suffered through his marriage causing a change of thought and heart.

Accordingly, if you stop reading the Bible, a person loses the constant affirmation of God and his promises. This had not been the first friend of mine who had stopped living according to the Bible's principles. Even when my friend had stopped coming to church, I felt sad about his predicament and his choice in life. That dream was a way of telling me about what had happened to his heart and mind. For quite awhile, I believed some kind of spark still existed inside him that could be reignited. More so than that, the dream gave me insight into some stories of the Bible that had been confusing until this dream opened up the subject of the importance of belief in our lives.

Dreams are a powerful way for God to speak to man. The dreams experienced by people in the Bible are very vivid and explained in detail. I know that when my dreams are very vivid, I must pay attention to them and try to understand what message lies within the dream. Because dreams come true in my life, I tend to want to think that destiny is not such a farfetched idea.

My intense dream was very vivid. I could literally see the veins inside of the demons wings even in the darkness. Meditating on this dream chose to be of great value as God directed my thought toward the book of JOB. Little did I know my dream would have a profound meaning beyond anything I had ever known.

One thing I do not want people to believe is that demons are anywhere near the description in my dream. I have read many books portraying demons in many different ways. I believe this is one way that I am comfortable in order to come to an understanding they were demons.

I call them demons, but they are fallen angels according to scripture. The Bible talks about a third of the heaven's angels leaving to be with Satan as he was thrown to earth, which became his domain.

When angels have approached humans in the Bible, they appeared to be similar to humans because those that encountered them immediately accepted them. If they had looked like Jar Jar Binks from the Star Wars Trilogy, I do not believe people would have bowed down to them in such humility. They probably would have run away seeking out their local psychiatrist to see if they were going crazy.

Why is my dream important? I had never really thought very deeply about the plans of Satan who is in opposition to God. My thoughts were about circumstances in my life that proved God was listening and that Satan was trying to intervene in that communication whether by physical or spiritual means. My car breaks down, I attribute it to Satan wanting me to get angry. The communication between my wife and I is severed for some uncanny reason and Satan has disturbed the real meaning of the words being said. My depth of Satan's attacks had been narrowed to quick hits here and there because that is all the time Satan had to attack anyone.

For some reason people believe that once the physical harm came to JOB through the compilation of events by removing his family, prosperity, and eventually exhibiting boils, sores on his body, that Satan stopped at that point, and gave up. Through my disturbing dream, I realized that was just the beginning of Satan's attacks on JOB. Satan was targeting JOB's belief because if Satan could change JOB's belief and make JOB believe differently about his relationship with God, JOB would be broken.

The first level of attack Satan was able to attain was to do everything to JOB but harm him. The second level of attack deepened and God told Satan the only thing he had to do was spare his life. He could not kill JOB. Everything else, and that means everything else, except death, was at Satan's disposal. Satan did not stop at just the physical aspect of attacking JOB, but now, the spiritual and mental attacks were also included. Satan's intent was to remove JOB's belief using his friends that came to him in his troubles.

I was always bothered by the idea that the two chapters of devastation JOB experienced was the precursor to the 36 chapters of someone trying to console JOB. This is not the case. Within the 36 chapters lies a new perspective to think about. These chapters are not about JOB's friends having compassion and trying to console him, but Satan's attacks on the very core of JOB's belief about God. I found nothing in the chapters by JOB's friends that relate any form of compassion. If I had compassion for someone in the way JOB's friends had compassion on him, I would not have any friends at all. The funny part is that in my effort to convey Jesus to people who have no understanding of who Jesus is and what Jesus did is similar to JOB's friends responses.

So, I immediately tested the theory that the 36 chapters were of an attacking nature. I was surprised to find out what I learned through the wisdom in the disturbing dream that I was right. A pattern exists in the responses to JOB by his friends. The following chapters will expose the foundation more clearly about a systematic approach to the attack that nearly worked. This new perspective has some great wisdom, and at the same time, some challenges in the way we think about religious doctrine.

Through this experience of dreams and reading JOB, I realize that the core idea of becoming a disciple for God lies in the change of beliefs a person has compiled throughout their lifetime. Many beliefs are made up to deal with circumstances and problems either by other people or by ourselves. Many people do not believe there is a God. Some of those people study the Bible and change their belief. Belief is the strongest aspect of our lives. What are the beliefs we hold to and why do we hold to them and drive our lives in the directions they go?

Before I became a disciple, my belief was grounded in my intelligence. I did not need a God. I graduated top 10 in my high school, so I knew I possessed intelligence to guide my life without the need for the wisdom that people following the Bible had. I now know the wisdom I believed was ludicrous.

Some of the stories that stopped me from seeking wisdom in the Bible came from seeing Christian pastors buying million dollar homes attaining it from the people that supported his ministry. This was after the people were told they should give because God commanded that the pastor live in such a home. I know there are Catholics who are sincere in their faith, but the multitudes of stories of child molestation through the Catholic faith churned my stomach. It still does because those in positions of power hide such godlessness from the authorities. They will not find their reward in heaven because they have subjected children to these circumstances knowingly. They have harmed children not directly, but indirectly and as God states in **Matthew 18:6** "*If anyone causes one of these little ones—those who believe in me—to stumble, it would be **better** for them to have a large millstone hung around their neck and to be drowned in the depths of the sea.*"

I sought out Buddha and Taoism, Hinduism, and studied a little Islam as well. Each of these did not convince me to follow God. Therefore, I chose to stay away from all religious institutions.

Now you ask how my beliefs changed. The story is unusual. I am going to do something I have seen only a few times written in anyone's book. I am going to write about my conversion. I am doing it mainly because the conversion was dramatic and I have not heard any other stories even close to what I experienced. After the event took place, I spoke about it to a variety of people and they commented that it was a "radical saving" or "radical awakening." I tend to believe this because of my situation. I was 32 years old, never had a girlfriend, never married, unrelatable, and very twisted in my mind and heart. I needed a big slap.

I was in my car driving down Rodeo Drive in Beverly Hills. I noticed something unusual coming from the entrance to Gap for Kids. I looked over and saw a girl whose beauty radiated from the door as she greeted people coming in the front door. I found a parking spot and proceeded to Gap for Kids. I needed to buy my niece a Christmas present anyway.

As I entered the store, an unusually friendly girl named Suzanne greeted me. I did some shopping and on the way out, I started talking to her. I asked her out for coffee. She said she dates only people in her church. I said "oh." To which she replied, "But you can come to church if you want." Well, I had about 4 years as a child in an Episcopalian Church and knew many of the stories of the Bible, so I told her I would go. Her beauty had coerced me to be open to something I was not normally open to doing.

Upon entering the church, which happened to be on the 17th floor of a high-rise building in Los Angeles, I was surprised to see and feel there was something different. People were happy. I had not seen this before.

I lived a large portion of my life in Reno, Nevada until I moved. I met a guy who went to my rival high school in Reno. I met a person with the last name of Reno. The table was set. It was a midweek service overlooking the city. The view was stunning. We broke up into groups that separated guys from girls. In this group, the conversation between the guys befuddled me. I could hear they were speaking English, but could not understand a word they were saying. They might as well have been speaking Chinese for all it mattered. The conversation was unnerving to say the least because I thought I was an intelligent human being, and I was totally clueless as to what they were talking about. I was asked to study the Bible to which I told myself, "If I don't study, the girl I met will find out, and that will be that." I studied for what seemed a long time. Everyone kept telling me I was not getting it. I did not understand the Bible.

I was tired of hearing I did not understand the Bible and proceeded to meditate about what I was being taught because, really, I just wanted others to believe I could understand. Then it happened. I went through a transformation, through a powerful unexplainable experience I could only attribute to something I could not see, touch, feel, or smell. I talked to several people about the experience and found out only a few had something similar, but not as intense. I certainly needed something radical to shake my beliefs.

I hesitate to put into words what my experience was on the basis that there are those who will not believe it. Here it goes anyway. I was lying in my bed with music from Yanni playing to relax me. I started thinking about all I had been learning. I went through the process to confirm to myself that I heard the word, I believed the word, I confessed my sins, and I was in the process of repenting of those sins I became aware of. I knew I needed to be baptized, but something was missing. Then I remember someone telling me to forgive. So, being very tired of thinking about all the Bible stuff, I said, "Forgive? I forgive everyone for everything that has ever been done to me. I am just tired of thinking and trying to understand."

Then it happened. As I lay on the bed, my eyes went blind. I could not see out of them at all. A couple of seconds later, somehow I was given vision in a different way and was able to see the entire room, all 360 degrees at once, without my eyes. I was starting to feel a little fear creep in. I entertained the thought I had died, which freaked me out. As I lay there, I felt what seemed to be a knife or some sharp-edged instrument cut through my body from my head to my toe right down the center of my chest. This split in half what seemed to be a shell about 6 inches thick made of clear dirty plastic that was around my body. The two halves separated for about a second and then flew off into oblivion in opposite directions.

I suddenly felt light as a feather as if I was going to float away. I thought I had died at this point. I grabbed the bed trying to stay put. Suddenly, something hit my head that felt like wet paint was dripping on my head and down my body, inside and out defying gravity; and may I remind you I was lying horizontal on the bed. The substance finished down to my toes and I experienced a burst of energy. I lost the 360-degree vision and the normal vision in my eyes came back.

As I lay there listening to the music playing, I realized the sound of the music had changed. I could hear every detail in the song. I sat up in bed to gather my wits. I stood up and tried to walk to the doorway. As I tried to walk to the door, my leg swung out from under me and completely out of control. I fell to the ground and grabbed the doorframe to stop me. The feeling was as if someone had been causing resistance on my legs and now the resistance was gone. The amount of energy used to move the restricted leg must have been a lot. By using that same energy to move the leg, the one that was freed from restriction, caused my leg to go way up in the air as I fell to the floor. I felt like a baby trying to walk again without the diapers. The amount of energy I had inside was amazing. I believed I could run a marathon, and it would not have bothered me.

The next day, a few of my friends were studying the Bible with me after church at a Carls Jr. I told them about the incident, which caused some uneasiness with them. I sat down, opened the Bible, and was going to read a little until they gathered their lesson and thoughts. I do not remember where I opened the Bible, but when I started to read, certain words fell away from the page and what was left was, "Hi, it's about time you arrived. Listen, we are going to fill your head with so much knowledge you are going to freak out, as you are doing right now." I jumped up and yelled, "THE BIBLE IS TALKING TO ME. THE BIBLE IS TALKING TO ME." My friends told me to sit down because I was embarrassing them in the restaurant. I experienced that same situation several times during the next two years. But, the most amazing part is that the Bible now made sense to me.

I attribute the experience to what the Bible says about opening up a person's mind so they can understand the scriptures in Luke 24:45. If I could not understand the scriptures, there is no way I could understand who God was, or what I am to do with that information. Also, my change came with power as in 1 Thessalonians 1:4-6 *"For we know, brothers and sisters loved by God, that he has chosen you, because our gospel came to you not simply with words but also with power, with the Holy Spirit and deep conviction."* It took this powerful experience to unlock my mind to mold my heart.

At this point, I knew I had changed dramatically. When the incident happened, my beliefs changed as well. I now knew for a fact that something existed I could not explain with words, which came by thinking about words, and that being God. Through studying the Bible and contemplating what was being taught, my beliefs changed. I needed that unexplainable experience embedded on my mind and heart because remembering that experience helped me to stay on course with remaining in the faith.

By the way, I never did date Suzanne, but I did learn how to date with pure motives. Four years later I met my wife.

The most important change that affected my life was the ability to understand the Bible. I could not understand the Bible before this event took place, and then after the event, the Bible made complete sense to me. The words and context of the paragraphs came to life. My mind had been unlocked in a way that was inconceivable. I was in awe at the sudden change of understanding. The change of understanding made no sense to me though. How could the radical event open my mind as it did? I was purposely blocked from understanding before the event and after the event, my beliefs were different.

My beliefs about religion had been rooted in the exposed evil deeds within the religious systems, which I turned into reasons for not opening up to God. I used people's sin as an excuse to be closed minded toward God.

During my time researching and meditating on the new perception about JOB, I realize there is a force I am dealing with trying to break my belief in God, in myself, and in others. A variety of circumstances has had the power to break my concentration on God and came close to destroying my belief on several occasions. Only by seeking God, believing he will rescue me, his promises, opening up to others in the faith, and praying, have my beliefs remained grounded in the precious relationship with God.

I am not even close to being like JOB, but I can learn from JOB. The intense persecution by a satan-induced attack by JOB's friends, and the strength that JOB displayed, leaves me to believe there was no one like JOB. JOB's beliefs about God were strong and grounded. Satan was out to break JOB's beliefs and prove JOB was not worthy of being lifted up by God. The next chapter will expose the foundation and show that Satan did not stop after the first two chapters in JOB.

The Unseen Figure

Shortly after his father died, John awoke in the middle of the night sweating profusely and shaking. Renee felt the bed shake while groans of agony emanated from John's direction. She turned to ask if he was all right. As he lay there trembling in fear, he was able to squeak out a few words describing a dark figure approaching him from the bedroom doorway. He quickly dismissed it as a nightmare and went back to sleep. Several nights later, the dark figure appeared even closer to their bed, only this time, John was sure he was awake. He quickly turned on the light, but the figure was gone.

Experiences such as these are a common occurrence in the lives of many people. They are portrayed in stories that permeate society whether by movies, books, or news articles. Some people love to think about evil and watch horror movies. Others find it a waste of time. Still others fear thinking about evil.

People that experience dark figures coming into their lives without invitation explain in detail a variety of circumstances. Dark figures come without faces, seen out of the corners of people's eyes, clawing the backs of people, knocking on bedroom doors, walking down stairways, walking in cemeteries, and speaking words. Some individuals have been scared to the point of seeking psychological help. Whatever the circumstance, dark figures have an impact from our experience of them.

The belief is that most people desire to be good, which causes evil to be elusive and difficult to understand. Elements commonly associated with evil involve unbalanced behavior involving expediency (a regard for what is politic or advantageous rather than for what is right or just; a sense of self-interest), selfishness, ignorance, or neglect. Evil can be the catalyst that drives people to commit murder, cause mayhem, jealousy, anger, fear, rage and other bad character traits. A villain is known as the antagonist in opposition to the hero. However, evil in a story creates movement and balance.

Authors create some incredibly evil people in their stories. To get a feel for the dark side, here are a few memorable lines from stories:

American Psycho: Patrick Bateman said, "My pain is constant and sharp and I do not hope for a better world for anyone. In fact, I want my pain to be inflicted on others. I want no one to escape."

The Lion, The Witch and the Wardrobe: The White Witch said, "You know that every traitor belongs to me as my lawful prey and that for every treachery I have a right to a kill... And so, that human creature is mine. His life is forfeit to me. His blood is my property."

Harry Potter And The Half-Blood Prince: Voldemort said, "I can make bad things happen to people who annoy me. I can make them hurt if I want to."

Dracula: Count Dracula said, "My revenge has just begun! I spread it over centuries and time is on my side."

The Silence Of The Lambs: Hannibal Lecter said, "A census taker tried to quantify me once. I ate his liver with some fava beans and a big Amarone."

Paradise Lost: Satan said, "Better to reign in Hell, then serve in Heav'n."

Dark figures are not the only figures seen by people or written about in stories. Other figures are attributed to having seen angels. There are thousands of stories of seeing angels whether awake or in a dream. But, how do we tell the difference between angels and dark figures of evil since 2 Corinthians 11:12-15 tells us "...*And no wonder, for* **Satan himself masquerades as an angel of light**." It is not surprising, then, if Satan also masquerades as a servant of righteousness. Where do we draw the fine line? In order to understand the specific passage of JOB that sheds light on the book of JOB, this differentiation between evil and good spirits needs to be understood.

Let us start with some passages from the Bible that describe the actions of angels. I do this because I have not read any earlier descriptions of angels. The following passages do not encompass all the scriptures describing angels, but only a few I believe are important in our discussion. In the Old Testament, the phrase "the angel of the Lord" or "the angel of God" prefaces most of the occasions when angels speak to people. The other instances describe an angel that will perform some act whether in the Old or New Testament. Angels came to carry out orders from God.

In Genesis 16, Hagar carries on a conversation with an angel. The angel told Hagar she will have decedents too numerous to count because Sarai, Abraham's wife, had mistreated her. In Genesis 19, angels appear to Lot, come into his house, and ate with Lot. Angels appeared in a dream on a stairway. In Exodus 3, an angel appeared in the flames of a fire within a bush. In Number 22, an angry God sent an angel to stand in the road to oppose travelers. A donkey saw the angel with a sword in his hand and turned off the road. In Judges 2, an angel speaks to the Israelites.

Judges 6:12
When the **angel** of the Lord appeared to Gideon,

Judges 6:21
Then the **angel** of the Lord touched the meat and the unleavened bread with the tip of the staff that was in his hand. Fire flared from the rock, consuming the meat and the bread. And the **angel** of the Lord disappeared.

Judges 13:6
Then the woman went to her husband and told him, "*A man of God came to me. He looked like an **angel** of God, very awesome.*"

Judges 13:16
The **angel** of the Lord replied, "Even though you detain me, I will not eat any of your food.

1 Kings 19:5
Then he lay down under the bush and fell asleep. All at once an **angel** touched him and said, "Get up and eat."

Hosea 12:4
He struggled with the **angel** and overcame him; he wept and begged for his favor.

Zechariah 2:3
While the **angel** who was speaking to me was leaving, another **angel** came to meet him

Matthew 2:13
When they had gone, an **angel** of the Lord appeared to Joseph in a dream. "Get up," he said, "take the child and his mother and escape to Egypt.

Acts 10:4

Cornelius stared at him in fear. "What is it, Lord?" he asked. The **angel** answered, "Your prayers and gifts to the poor have come up as a memorial offering before God.

Acts 12:9-**10**
And he went out, and followed him; and did not know that what was done by the angel was real but thought he was seeing a vision. When they were past the first and the second guard posts, they came to the iron gate that leads to the city; which opened to them of its own accord: and they went out, and went down one street; and immediately the angel departed from him.

People still claim to see angels. Instances show up in a variety of areas and situations. An article about the crash of flight 93 depicted a person seeing angels appear. A white mist started out and began to take shape in the form of angels. Individuals with advanced educational degrees claim to have seen angels when they were children.

Some have written books after collecting hundreds of eyewitness accounts from intelligent people claiming to have experienced contact with angels. Angels have come in many forms. These forms include very pretty girls, large men with wings, angels that look similar to us, and many have seen more than one angel at a time. Even Paul states in Hebrews 13:2, *"Do not neglect to show hospitality to strangers, for by this some have entertained angels without knowing it."*

The difference between angels and dark evil figures is concluded in Hebrews 1:14 *"Are they not all ministering spirits sent forth to minister for those who will inherit salvation?"* Angels are sent to minister to us, not accuse us, confuse us, or anger us. They are sent for our good, for our redemption, for our salvation, and all because God loves us. They are there to protect us, help us, lead us, and confirm that God is listening. Most importantly, they are seen by us if

God so wishes for us to see them. They do not hide themselves and convey messages to us as dark angels or Satan himself would do.

In JOB 4, Eliphaz describes a visitation by a dark form. I believe Satan himself visited Eliphaz in a dream. The visitation more than likely happened while the friends were waiting to talk to JOB. This visit laid the foundation for Eliphaz's conversation with JOB, which led the way toward an onslaught of accusations in an effort to get JOB to see, believe, and repent of his sin Obviously, Eliphaz was not aware JOB had not sinned.

The course of statements of accusations between JOB's friends took on a specific path attacking from every angle possible. Satan knew that if JOB broke and changed his belief about his innocence of sin, this would break JOB's faith in God by causing confusing and conflicting thoughts within JOB's mind and heart. I believe breaking our belief is Satan's main goal. The physical challenges we have in our life is only a drop in a bucket compared to the attacks made on our beliefs about God. This is the drive of the conversation for 36 chapters in JOB – breaking our belief system. The dark form started the attack.

In order to test whether or not Satan did not quit after the physical harm to JOB, I need to point to the particular scripture in JOB that describes a very familiar scene a multitude of people have experienced in their lives – not exactly the same way, but similar.

The scene in JOB is similar to a scene we find in Genesis where Satan set in motion certain thinking patterns for an individual to believe a certain way by questioning their knowledge and led them to believe differently. A dark figure visits Eliphaz while he sleeps and gives him two questions reaffirming what he already believes but is the catalyst to an attack of doctrinal pounding in an effort to break JOB's belief.

JOB 4 - Eliphaz
A word was secretly brought to me,
   my ears caught a whisper of it.
Amid **disquieting dreams in the night**,
   when deep sleep falls on people,
fear and trembling seized me
   and made all my bones shake.
A spirit glided past my face,
   and the hair on my body stood on end.
It stopped,
   but I could not tell what it was.
A form stood before my eyes,
   and I heard a hushed voice:
'Can a mortal be more righteous than God?
   Can even a strong man be more pure than his Maker?

New American Standard Bible (©1995)
Can mankind be just before God? Can a man be pure before his Maker?

Holman Christian Standard Bible (©2009)
Can a person be more righteous than God, or a man more pure than his Maker?

International Standard Version (©2012)
Can a mortal person be more righteous than God? Or can the purity of the valiant exceed that of his maker?

Douay-Rheims Bible
Shall man be justified in comparison of God, or shall a man be more pure than his maker?

Young's Literal Translation
Is mortal man than God more righteous? Than his Maker is a man cleaner?

JOB 4 (cont.)
If God places no trust in his servants,
   if he charges his angels with error,
how much more those who live in houses of clay,
   whose foundations are in the dust,
   who are crushed more readily than a moth!
Between dawn and dusk they are broken to pieces;
   unnoticed, they perish forever.
Are not the cords of their tent pulled up,
   so that they die without wisdom?'"

      Satan visits Eliphaz in a dream. In JOB 4:15, Eliphaz is expressing the dream he had and the spirit that came to see him. He could not see the spirit because the spirit was only a form that stood before him. Eliphaz was seized in fear and trembling because of not knowing what was standing before him. Obviously, whatever was standing in front of him did not want to be seen or known. It was hidden in the darkness. All that could be heard was a voice and that voice wanted Eliphaz to understand man cannot be more righteous than God.

      Eliphaz is reciting what Satan has expressed to him in the dream. Eliphaz believes what he hears is correct and true because of the understanding about God's laws and regulations. And, who would know more about being charged with error than Satan himself.

      The statement *"Can a mortal be more righteous than God? Can even a strong man be more pure than his Maker?"* is an accusatory statement. Satan was accusing JOB of being more righteous than God is. JOB therefore had to be in sin of some sort. And, yes, we can be blind to sin such as pride

(Psalm 36), selfishness, etc. where another person needs to help us acknowledge our wrongdoing. This is exactly what Satan wanted Eliphaz to think – JOB is in sin and he is too prideful to admit it.

If we look at the statement "*If God places no trust in his servants*" and realize the twisting of the phrase to encourage the thought that God does not trust, we can see Satan's ploy in convincing Eliphaz of certain thoughts. The first was a question 'Can a mortal be more righteous than God?' is answerable with a no. The second question, 'Can even a strong man be more pure than his Maker?' is answerable with a no. Therefore, the third question will follow in line with the first two with an answerable "no, God does not trust his servants."

We see a pattern evolve to convince Eliphaz of elements of God's law that are not quite true. Then Satan drives in the idea that even angels cannot get away from God and his judgment of error of which JOB is obviously misunderstanding because he is made of dust ("*how much more things made of dust*").

Allegations and accusations of error have been sweetly driven into Eliphaz's heart and thought patterns. Error is exactly what Satan wants Eliphaz to believe about JOB – JOB is in error and in sin. This thinking is the basis for which the four friends charge JOB with allegations of unrighteousness contained within the next 36 chapters. The 36 chapters are not an expression of compassion from JOB's friends.

God was well known throughout the Israelite community as blessing those that follow God's laws who try to stay out of sin and repent from committed sin. Those that did not repent were not blessed. This type of thinking permeated the Israelites in determining the separation from the people of God and those not of God. This is the religious doctrine of those days and exists today in many religious cultures.

Eliphaz has an experience with a spirit and describes the entity as a spirit not an angel. Whenever an angel made contact with humans, it was stated as so. Eliphaz is frightened by the spirit to the point of his bones shaking.

Since Satan was trying to break JOB of his faith in God, Satan had to equip JOB's friends with the idea that JOB was in sin. If you remember, God gave Satan permission to do anything *"except" take JOB's life."* The statement gives a lot of leeway to strategize advancement toward breaking JOB. This fits into the pattern of tormenting JOB to the point of breaking his will and most importantly an attempt to break his belief.

Let us look at the correlation between the statements Eliphaz makes and the statements from Satan in the Garden of Eden.

Genesis 3
Now the serpent was more crafty than any of the wild animals the LORD God had made. He said to the woman, *"Did God really say, 'You must not eat from any tree in the garden'?"* The woman said to the serpent, *"We may eat fruit from the trees in the garden, but God did say, 'You must not eat fruit from the tree that is in the middle of the garden, and you must not touch it, or you will die.'"* *"You will not certainly die,"* the serpent said to the woman. *"For God knows that when you eat from it your eyes will be opened, and you will be like God, knowing good and evil."* In the Garden of Eden, Satan questions the truth about what God said. "Did God really say…" opens the door for someone to question what was actually said by God.

In JOB, Satan does not question whether God had said what He said, Satan confirms to Eliphaz that God's laws are absolutely right, and man cannot be above God and make his own laws or be purer than God. Living a life by the laws of God does not always mean you will live a good life though. God's laws point out our impurity and sin. We are meant to suffer mainly because of our impurity. We need to work to remove our impurity so it can be replaced with something much greater as Romans 5:2-4 says, *"And we boast in the hope of the glory of God. Not only so, but we also glory in our sufferings, because we know that suffering produces perseverance; perseverance, character; and character, hope."*

The statement by Satan to Eliphaz is accusatory of JOB being in sin. Because it was an accusatory statement, this sets the dividing line that is needed to differentiate between angels and demons or Satan. Satan himself charged JOB of wrongdoing to Eliphaz. Therefore, an angel of God cannot be considered as the dark figure who visited Eliphaz.

Bildad acknowledges his understanding of the accusation by restating Eliphaz's statement in JOB 25:4 *"How then can a mortal be righteous before God? How can one born of woman be pure?"* Eliphaz and Bildad both were driven into mis-judgment.

Being mis-judged is very hurtful and damages people deeply. Many people judge very quickly about all kinds of situations and circumstances. Being mis-judged damages our beliefs about people and that is exactly what Satan wants to target – beliefs. People can be mis-judged in their attitudes, appearances, communications, intentions, and a whole collection of other things causing strife in each other's life.

A couple I will call Bob and Mary had been married for about 10 years when out of the blue the mother of the wife, I will call Nancy, started acting strange. Up to this point, Bob and Mary had gone out of their way to serve Nancy and her fiancé, as Jesus would do, in order to try to live out their lives as disciples.

Mary would ask Bob to help her mother repair or fix computer issues, move furniture, and generally do what he could especially since Nancy and her fiancé were well into their years and did not have the strength or experience to do many things.

Mary spent time with her mom going places and helping with certain tasks as well as enjoying each other's company. Bob and Mary would spend holidays with Nancy and her fiancé and make time to see them at least every week or two since they only lived a few miles away. For nine years, the relationship had been deepening between Bob and Mary and Nancy and her fiancé, and it seemed to be getting better and better.

Mary and Nancy made it part of their routine to go to a special spot every year about the same time around mother's day to enjoy being together. Nancy set up a time to go to their favorite place, but one year when the time came to experience the time together, circumstances came up, which pushed the date out a little further.

Nancy called Mary and was consumed with anger expressing that Mary did not desire to be with her. Mary was overwhelmed with sorrow because her mother felt this way, and it was not the truth. Shortly afterward, the second date came up and Mary called to arrange a meeting; however, her mother was still angry and did not want to go. Mary tried to get her mother to express what was really on her mind so they could get it out and move on, but it only got worse. Eventually, the communication became so bad Mary had to stop all communications with her mom because of the attitudes.

Some time later, an email was sent by Nancy, who stated Bob was a thief and a liar. Bob and Mary were astonished Nancy had judged Bob to be a thief and a liar for some unknown reason?

Mary was devastated to hear her mother had such a mis-judging attitude about Bob who had done no wrong at all. The damage of mis-judgment fell upon Mary who was deeply hurt. After everything Bob and Mary had done to serve Nancy and her fiancé, to be treated in such a way was a horrific experience – all because of mis-judgment.

In churches, we rely so much on preachers to bring the truth to us that we do not question their truthfulness by our own comprehension of the Bible. We just accept what they say as truth. But, how could they be wrong since they are supposed to know the Bible? We relinquish our rights as followers of Christ through our own laziness or procrastination or whatever stops us by accepting "they must be right since they are better studied than we are."

Preachers can be wrong, but how would we know unless we dig into the Bible ourselves and come to an understanding of what we are reading? Preachers can be preaching messages and at the same time be steeped in sin. The Catholic Church is a good example of this through the acceptance of the detestable sin of allowing sex with children by only moving sinful clergy to another church instead of bringing them to justice.

Leaders in Christian churches are no different. Stories of adultery, lying, and selfish gains permeate the atmosphere. Even in the church I go to there have been instances of pure sin on the part of the leaders. The good thing in our church culture is that people question what leaders say from the pulpit because it affects the entire church, especially when something is said just a little bit off truth, which is similar to the way Satan presented the truth to Eliphaz.

In 1 John 4:1 *"Dear friends, do not believe every spirit, but test the spirits to see whether they are from God, because many false prophets have gone out into the world."* We are to test the spirits of everyone, especially a leader. If a leader, who has been speaking while in a good spirit gets tempted and decides to sin, how will you know if what he is saying is truth now?

The leader needs to repent (openly confess his sins and turn away from) and people need to know what he has done. If they do not know what he has done, the truth is distorted because the spirit is being darkened. This hiding of sin is the reason why we need to know whether or not leaders are speaking the truth by our own understanding of the Bible.

Everyone hides sin at times in his or her life. The amount of time the sin is hidden varies. We can be prideful in our sin, which is why Eliphaz was so adamant about JOB repenting. He felt JOB was being prideful about his situation.

The fact is we are all like Eliphaz too. We think we know things because our intellect hears a fact and we accept and believe we now know the truth. Testing the words of spirits is not an easy task. We all fall short all the time. It is no excuse for not knowing what the God you worship expects from you and whether others are telling the truth. Leaders are not more holy than anyone else is. Those that have been baptized have the Holy Spirit.

To simply accept someone else's understanding about what the Bible says is to be like the virgins in Matthew 25 The Parable of the Ten Virgins. All ten were waiting for the bridegroom. Five of the virgins were too lazy to get oil for their lamps. The funny thing is when the virgins came back, the bridegroom did not say, "oh, now you have your oil." Well, it is too late. The room is full." The bridegroom said, "*I do not know you.*" All ten virgins were in the same place, heard the same message about the bridegroom coming, but five were lazy and did not take time to understand what was expected by the bridegroom.

When we hear messages preached from the pulpit, we retain about 10 percent of what we hear. People today who are similar to the five virgins without oil obviously rely on that 10 percent they hear and do not dig in to the Bible themselves to find out what is expected – and that being oil for their lamps.

By relying on other people's knowledge of the Bible as a sure way to get to heaven is a myth. We must know the contents of the Bible so that we can know our creator personally. I cannot have a relationship with a friend's friend if I have never taken the time to know them. I also conclude that "just" reading the Bible does not give you special privileges to knowing God. You must read the Bible yourself, come to an understanding of who God is and what he expects from you, and then do what is expected. This also helps you test the spirits and the words of those speaking to ensure you have the oil necessary to get to heaven.

The saying that "once you are connected to God through Christ, you are assured a way into heaven" is a myth. Being connected to Christ is the beginning of a journey that includes pitfalls and testing by God to change your character to be more like Christ. To this, we give our hearts, minds, and souls.

Many of us will be tested by the dark figure talking to us in our sleep, awake, or by our friends. JOB was tested by his friends and did not sin in the process. This is an amazing feat of knowing himself and God. We must find a way to be as JOB, and the more we study the Bible, the more we can understand what it takes.

When we sin, we feel the guilt. We understand as JOB and his friends did in JOB 11:13-15 "*Yet if you devote your heart to him and stretch out your hands to him, if you put away the sin that is in your hand and allow no evil to dwell in your tent, then, **free of fault**, you will lift up your face.*" God honors righteousness.

Rebellion toward God equals pain, which is a core belief of the Israelite and Christian communities. Our beliefs are at the center of what we know about God to be true. Our beliefs are constantly being challenged. Our faith, which is worth more than gold, is constantly being refined by the fire and tested by dark figures. It is up to us to respond righteously with a wisdom that comes from God.

If Satan has a main goal to break our belief of God in our life, what are the tools used to do this? How is the attack manifested toward JOB? How is the attack manifested in our own lives? Why would God allow us to be attacked when he is supposed to put a hedge around us and protect us? How would our faith be developed if we were not allowed to be attacked?

Break the Man

"till at last the child's mind is these suggestions, and the sum of the suggestions is the child's mind. And not the child's mind only. The adult's mind too all his life long. The mind that judges and desires and decides made up of these suggestions. But all these suggestions are our suggestions!" - Aldous Huxley

If I were to think about breaking a man down, the obvious things come first. Removing the physical aspects of comfort, seclusion to a solitary area, little or no contact with other humans for a period of time, torture, and repetition are some of the ideas I have seen in movies. I certainly would not want to have someone try to break me down in any of these ways. However, we are under attack every day either by our own hearts and minds, by others, by Satan himself, or by God trying to train us to be the people he wants us to be. If we are a Christian, we certainly want to be broken down by God so he can transform our lives to be more like Jesus. How do we tell the difference between being broken down by God and Satan's attacks?

The most common view of breaking down a man includes brainwashing, mind altering, changing the beliefs of someone in order to insert new beliefs or ways of thinking. What does brainwashed, mind altering, and belief changing mean? All of them imply a person was presented with and bought into another set of beliefs whether false or true. A person's existing belief will repel any new beliefs, so a process of removing the arguments associated with their beliefs as well as removing the security of having the belief must take place to change their beliefs. We can also be easily brainwashed by remaining ignorant.

All of us want security in our lives. We want secure jobs, secure relationships, secure health, and secure freedom.

We define what we believe security to be in our lives. If having a cell phone creates security, then we will work to have a cell phone at all times. If owning a business creates security for someone, he or she will work to have a business.

I remember when I was a little boy learning to cope with the world. I had a favorite blanket that would go with me wherever I went. Life was good as long as I had that blanket. Admitting that as a man is not an easy thing to do, but I use it here as an example of how physical objects affect our security.

As a child and while on a trip to see Grandpa and Grandma, I had unknowingly left my favorite blanket behind at their house. About 50 miles or so into the trip, I noticed I was missing something that was very important to me. My mind went immediately into chaos mode, and I started crying over the absence of my security blanket. My dad had to turn around, adding time to an already four-hour trip to retrieve my blanket so I would stop crying.

Even at an early age, what we feel and see become very important to us. The objects we choose to associate ourselves with become very important. This importance stems from our beliefs in what makes us secure and satisfied. Of course, negative beliefs stem from negative events.

When the craving of security goes too far is when we go a little out-of-whack. Television shows us the detrimental affect this type of security has on people through shows such as animal hoarders or object hoarders. My daughter and son enjoy watching shows that portray a person having a multitude of animals for some reason. I use it to teach them having too many things is cause for reflection into why.

People also find security in food and come to a belief that eating the same food is the only food they are able to eat. When our beliefs have been damaged, the very thing we find security in is the thing breaking us down.

The most important and powerful way to break a man down is to be able to get to his belief system and change it. Just an attack on our physical being is not enough. This is the reason why JOB is a book in the Bible. JOB shows us how Satan is trying to break down our beliefs and security in God. We MUST understand Satan is after our core self – our beliefs.

Our belief system is the core of who we are. What we believe in becomes reality for us. I believe soccer is the greatest sport in the world because I enjoy playing and watching the game. The game is fast paced, physically challenging, takes a lot of talent to control a ball with your feet, and is emotionally charging.

My belief about country music started when I was a little kid. I did not like the sappy-everything-is-crashing-down-in-my-life songs. My belief of who I am was also constructed by the circumstances and events in my life that affected me on a deep level, as it does everyone's. Those with mis-beliefs, caused by events forcing us to believe in any number of detrimental ways, are what is keep psychology and psychiatry alive and well.

If I came to believe that frogs were evil and were very afraid of being around them, then I could ultimately end up with ranidaphobia. My belief becomes powerful enough to cause a terror so deep that I become paralyzed with fear over the sight of a frog. The power of belief is the strongest, most stable, powerful, earth moving, life changing aspect about being human. Beliefs are so strong that people are willing to die for a belief, as we know from the suicide bombers in the Middle East.

Beliefs give people the strength to conquer climbing Mount Everest. Whether negative or positive beliefs are the single most powerful thing a human has in their possession.

The first time I remember my mom saying she loved me was when I was 18 years old and going into the Marine

Corps. I had the weirdest feeling when she did because saying you loved someone was not a normal activity in our house; just the opposite was true. I do not remember her saying this word before that time. If she did say she loved me, which I am sure she said a few times, I do not remember. It was not enough for me to think otherwise. I knew she loved me because she took care of all four of us kids. However, saying "I love you" was not a constant phrase used. I certainly had not learned to respond with the same phrase back to my mom either. My belief about love had been loosely woven into my life. I had a skewed belief about love. Good job Satan. Now that I am grown, I say, "I love you" when I see or talk to her.

Our belief systems are being attacked at every angle and on a consistent basis. If we do not have a job, we are worthless. If we do not have a girl friend or wife, we are unlovable. If our parents do not pay attention to us, we are nothing to them. If God is not working in my life, God must have forgotten about me.

The way Satan attacked JOB was to remove everything physical around him, then using God's laws, using God's character, and using JOB's character as weapons through JOB's friends thereby challenging his security and belief in God. This is much different from the way man would break a man down.

Security in God is a double-edged sword. We want security that God will bring us into heaven when we die, but being too secure can cause us to become lax in our convictions about what it really takes to be a people of God, which is where Satan wants us to be – overly confident. Yes, love covers over sin, but God does not want us to become lazy. We must work and practice God's principles.

Sometimes, security in worldly things supersedes or becomes greater than security in God. JOB's security was not in worldly things. Satan resorted to the only aspect of

JOB that was left after he lost his physical things – his belief and security in God, as you will see in chapters that follow this one.

Our belief system changed when we came in contact with and made a commitment to God. We went from believing "there was no God" to "there is a God." Some have always believed in God but never did anything about this knowledge. They led a life unworthy of a people of God until one day their beliefs changed. Now, they work on being holy and righteous as well as learning to love.

Advertisers work very hard on the psyche of people in order to cause them to purchase certain products. Some ads work and some do not. The idea is to change people's beliefs that Pepsi is better than Coke, Republicans are better than Democrats – well, you get the point. Our beliefs are always being attacked at some level. Advertisers also know if a person is emotionally charged, they will not make rational decisions and are prone to making the decision to purchase a product.

Our beliefs can also change through knowledge that a group of people are all thinking the same way. Where is this more prevalent than in religious organizations? This is why the most important factor in making sure you are on the right path with God is to check and challenge the leaders of those organizations. We have to have a certain level of trust, but we cannot be afraid to question what is being said from the pulpit.

The mistaken belief that what is being said from the pulpit comes from God "IS" one of the most destructive beliefs Satan has worked very hard to ensure exists. Few people realize that preachers will not get you to heaven. They have their own path to step. You, yourself must get yourself to heaven through your knowledge and relationship with God. Just because you hear a preacher preach does not mean you will get to heaven. This is your journey, not the preacher's, and you must make sure you are on the right path by studying the Bible carefully coming to know God.

My grandmother was on her deathbed years ago. I knew she believed in God, but never went to church or practiced being a Christian in any way. I called her to try to get her to study the Bible with someone in her town and commit herself to God. My aunt called me and scolded me about what I had said to her – that she would not be with God after she died, which I did not say. My aunt did not go to church or study the Bible, but called a preacher she knew to get her answer.

The preacher told my aunt that my grandmother and my aunt would make it to heaven because of their belief in God. The preacher did not know my grandmother's life, what she believed, what she practiced, or how she lived. How could the preacher say such a thing?

The most destructive belief is that all you need to do is believe in God. Satan is doing well at securing this belief because of a single scripture John 3:16. This scripture is used by itself as the very doorway to God. Granted, a belief in God must exist before anything else happens, but it is not the only scripture necessary to go to heaven. Very few people take the entire passage John 3:1-16 and combine them together – because they are part of a whole concept – and see the commitment involved with following Jesus. Just "believe there is a God and you will be okay," is a lie. "...*Even the demons believe and shudder...*(James 2:19).

Much of our religious society has become like the study of the elephant. This work of Micheal Cohen gives a good example of what I am expressing. "An elephant was chained by its leg to a post to prevent it from straying. It hurt when it pulled on the chain so, in time, the elephant did not stray past the chain length thus avoiding the pain. A rope that the elephant could break was then used to replace the chain. The rope also triggered some pain so the elephant remained in place. The rope was removed and replaced over time by a string and finally nothing, but the elephant never went far enough from the post to discover it was free. Its psyche now contained the chain. It had been socialized not to stray."

Many of us have been socialized to believe all we need to do is believe in God and nothing more is expected. The pain of practicing to be righteous and faithful promotes this type of thinking because people do not like the pain it takes to change their lives. Pain causes people to resort to only believing and nothing more. The lie then becomes "As long as we believe in God, we can be secure that we will be brought to heaven when we die." However, this belief does not bring freedom as we see in the elephant story. By not challenging ourselves on a daily basis, we remain chained to the world of sin. French Philosopher Rousseau wrote, "Man is born free, but everywhere he is in chains."

When we only believe in God, then sin remains unchallenged, not removed, or repented of. It is believed that smoking and drinking excessively, lying, cheating, greed, sexual immorality can be atoned for by the simple belief in God. This is the reason why a 60% divorce rate exists – people believe they can do what they want in the marriage without consequence for their actions even though they love the other person or believe in God. Working on openness, righteousness, or humility does not exist. They "believe" in the marriage, but make no effort toward changing their own beliefs affecting their spouse. The marriage becomes a slow train riding on tracks toward the cliff of death.

When Satan succeeds in breaking our beliefs, we create new beliefs to replace the beliefs that were broken. These new beliefs are usually negative in nature. New beliefs like fear, shame, self-destruction, co-dependency, people pleasers, and so on come to fruition. Negative beliefs move us away from God even to the point of being Atheists.

I watched TV shows that depict someone at one time believing in God only to have an event take place in their life, which turns them into Atheists. This is the strength of JOB. He made it through his devastating event without sinning or turning away from God.

Many of you may not know there are step-by-step guides on how to change someone's mind. Many salespeople are well acquainted with the process. Getting rid of the wall of arguments by slowly chipping away until no arguments are left will get a sale. Satan uses this type of attack on JOB through JOB's friends. Presenting new arguments and debunking opposing arguments is the direction taken to change the mind or beliefs a person holds. Arguments are won because they are backed by solid facts and social proof with a repetitious attack. The new arguments are not necessarily true though.

As a young man, I worked as a pitchman for a company that sold rolling rulers at events such as county fairs or shows. I would stand in a booth for 12 hours a day selling rolling rulers. After doing a number of these events, I became very adapt at selling rulers.

One day I challenged myself to sell someone who had no need for a ruler whether for themselves or anyone they knew. I called a person from across the isle, did my three-minute pitch, and countered all the arguments presented, changed their belief, and made a profit. I was astounded at myself, but realized the power of what I did – and I am just human – just think what Satan is capable of doing in your life. The book "Screwtape Letters" by C.S. Lewis is a good example of this concept bringing to light what might possibly take place behind the scenes with demons and their strategy to disrupt belief systems.

Other ways of changing someone's mind or brainwashing includes triggering "what's in it for me," "attacking people's needs," "playing with people's emotions" and "persuasion with solutions," as 5Triggers.com states.

Making a connection between the new belief and the person takes quite a bit of walking on a tight rope. Playing with and using people's feelings are powerful. Advertisers have become well adapt at attacking and causing change in people all for a company's profit by convincing people to be consumers even if they do not have money to purchase.

This is the main reason why I do not want my children watching television – movies, without commercials, okay – but television – no! I know I cannot get rid of all of the advertisements, but a few are better than allowing ads to create a habit in my children of needing that emotional feeling from commercials, which end up turning my children into gullible consumers. We are habitual creatures and we can get addicted to commercials too.

Beliefs are attacked slowly, methodically, and with repetition. President Bush's staff were magnificent in changing our beliefs. First, propaganda was sent out in the form of a question. "What Does Weapons of Mass Destruction Mean for the Safety of the World?" This thought makes us think, "Wow, there must be weapons of mass destruction somewhere." Later, Iraq is linked to the question about the weapons. Soon, we are traveling down a path to a change in belief that Iraq has weapons of mass destruction and the world is not safe because of this. We then become okay with taking the weapons away from Iraq in the form of a war. The red herring was thrown at us, we took a bite, and many companies profited.

Repetition is the key to success in changing beliefs. Each successive expression of information is changed just a little to counter arguments and continue persuasion. We get a small glimpse of repetition used in JOB. We do not know how long the conversation lasted between JOB and his friends, but it was long enough to bring the important issues to light we must understand and become aware of in our lives.

How do we protect our belief system? First, we need to become aware of the strength our beliefs have in our life. Second, we need to understand our beliefs are being attacked daily and even hourly. Third, we need to stop reinforcing negative beliefs by whatever means possible. Fourth, we need to study the Bible to understand how to ground our beliefs in righteousness and faith. Fifth, we need to understand, as JOB experienced, just because God does not answer, he is still there with us (Isaiah 50:10). Finally, practicing righteousness and faith keeps our beliefs from being damaged or destroyed.

Protecting our belief system is our greatest responsibility. It is also our greatest challenge. If we have the belief that the love of God is enough to protect our beliefs, we have been fooled by the very belief itself. Certainly God will protect us as much as possible, but if we consistently make unrighteous and unfaithful decisions, Hebrews 10:26 says, "if we deliberately keep on sinning after we have received the knowledge of the truth, no sacrifice for sin is left, but only a fearful expectation of judgment and of raging fire that will consume the enemies of God." We become "enemies of God" and relinquish our protection by God from someone who has changed our beliefs.

Our beliefs are connected to the desire to be righteous or unrighteous. If we believe we can be unrighteous and still be okay with God, Satan wins. If we believe we can be righteous, and repent from our unrighteousness through confession and atonement, God will protect us until he sees fit to teach us more faith or wisdom by allowing us to be challenged.

So in the words of Winston Churchill "Never, never, never, never–in nothing, great or small, large or petty–never give in, except to convictions of honor and good sense."

God's Laws

From the beginning of Adam and Eve, humanity has been suffering. From Adam and Eve's disobedience, the pain in child bearing would be greatly increased, the ground would be cursed so that painful toil is required, and the labor to produce crops would involve *"the sweat of your brow"* (Genesis 3:17). Humanity brings punishment and suffering upon themselves either as a consequence of their sin or from God's judgment. This is exactly what JOB's friends believed, and ultimately encouraged by Satan, when he appeared as the dark figure expressing this truth. Through the years, people have believed that suffering is punishment from God for their sin and for the most part, that is right.

The belief that punishment through suffering comes from God is made plain throughout the Bible. The strongest example is in Leviticus 28 – Curses for Disobedience. Here are a few other verses to give us the same understanding.

Leviticus 26:18-21 "'If after all this you will not listen to me, I will punish you for your sins seven times over. I will break down your stubborn pride and make the sky above you like iron and the ground beneath you like bronze. Your strength will be spent in vain, because your soil will not yield its crops, nor will the trees of your land yield their fruit. "'If you remain hostile toward me and refuse to listen to me, I will multiply your afflictions seven times over, as your sins deserve.

Leviticus 26:23-24 "'If in spite of these things you do not accept my correction but continue to be hostile toward me, I myself will be hostile toward you and will afflict you for your sins seven times over.

Leviticus 26:40-42 "'But if they will confess their sins and the sins of their ancestors—their unfaithfulness and their hostility toward me, which made me hostile toward them so that I sent them into the land of their enemies—then when their uncircumcised hearts are humbled and they pay for their sin, I will remember my covenant with Jacob and my covenant with Isaac and my covenant with Abraham, and I will remember the land."

Another side to suffering is the belief that when we look at other people who are suffering, most of the time, we believe the suffering is caused by their own sin or some uncontrollable circumstance. On the opposite side is the belief that when WE suffer, that suffering is caused mostly by someone else and does not come from our own sin. We rarely see our own sin.

The blame game is one of the most destructive of all beliefs. Not taking responsibility for your sin that damages yourself or others is rampant in our society. Everyone blames someone else for his or her problems. Finding a person that takes responsibility for the damage they do to themselves or others, no matter what the consequences are, is like looking for a needle in a haystack. When we look at Jesus on the cross, he had no sin. However, he gives us the example of forgiveness for other's sins. Taking responsibility for the damage our sin has caused others and ourselves is necessary so forgiveness can be extended. Eliphaz takes the stance that JOB has suffered greatly because of sin he has not confessed.

The book of JOB is not only about JOB's suffering even though he suffered greatly. God had so much faith JOB would not break under the pressure that he allowed Satan to attack his core beliefs. The second point is that JOB was a unique individual and one to be imitated and honored because of his strength to ward off the attacks.

The first strategy of Satan was to get Eliphaz to talk about God's laws and how they operate because they are true. These laws include the idea that suffering equals God's punishing hand. Talking about God's laws and how they operate sets the foundation for the next step of the attack. This expression of the laws begins and continues throughout the book of JOB by JOB's friends.

Satan follows up his attack by JOB's friends using God's character as a weapon. The next step is the attack on JOB himself and his character as a human. Satan uses God's laws, character, and our own character as a weapon to attack our beliefs.

Obviously, we can count on God's laws and how they operate because they are from God. God is truth, love, and righteousness. This is the confusing part about JOB if we put faith in the laws and what God says. God said he will punish for sin, but JOB did not sin. So, we have to see that JOB was not punished at all by God. God will not punish anyone without being tangled in sin.

This story was purely about how Satan attacks us and how faithful JOB was by not sinning. It is also about Satan giving us strife for no reason. A few chapters on suffering and 36 chapters on conversation between JOB and his friends is enough to point to a different purpose for the book of JOB.

Eliphaz starts out by recognizing how many times JOB has counseled others when they stumbled or faltered. Eliphaz acknowledges his respect for JOB because he has helped many others in their time of need. By relating JOB's current state to the people JOB has helped, puts JOB in the same category as those he has helped. Eliphaz immediately declares JOB is not blameless *"Consider now: Who, being innocent, has ever perished? Where were the upright ever destroyed?"* (JOB 4:7). He also expresses God's judgments are not for the righteous, but for the wicked. Those who sow trouble are destroyed. If JOB was innocent, he would not perish. The wicked are eventually destroyed, as was the case with JOB. Because of JOB's alleged wickedness, who would he call upon or turn to? Who would answer him? However, JOB already knows all this and claimed he was without sin.

The dark figure came to Eliphaz in the night, and I am pretty sure Bildad, Zophar, and Elihu also heard about Eliphaz's encounter with the dark figure before they met with JOB or they encountered the dark figure themselves. They obviously heard it from Eliphaz when he first spoke up, but I am not sure that was the first time they had heard it from Eliphaz. If Eliphaz told them beforehand, all three could then agree or disagree on what was happening to JOB. All three could be on board with the direction to take in getting JOB to confess his sin and have God stop the punishment JOB was undergoing.

This is similar to all organizations and how they deal with situations, circumstances, with people, the organization itself, outside influences, or natural disturbances. All people get together to discuss the situation or circumstance beforehand and decide what to do to find a solution to the situations.

Coming from this view, we can see JOB's friends were on the same thought pattern when speaking to JOB. Here are some statements made by JOB's friends stating the facts about God's laws and the punishment for sin:

He thwarts the plans of the crafty,
   so that their hands achieve no success.

He catches the wise in their craftiness,
   and the schemes of the wily are swept away.

Darkness comes upon them in the daytime;
   at noon, they grope as in the night.

Blessed is the one whom God corrects;
so do not despise the discipline of the Almighty

For he wounds, but he also binds up;
he injures, but his hands also heal.

When your children sinned against him,
he gave them over to the penalty of their sin.
Such is the destiny of all who forget God;
so perishes the hope of the godless.

Surely, God does not reject one who is blameless
or strengthen the hands of evildoers.

JOB's friends keep hammering away at JOB in hopes of getting JOB to see he is in sin even with harsh statements such as: *"Resentment kills a fool and envy slays the simple."* and *"I myself have seen a fool taking root, but suddenly his house was cursed."* Basically, they were calling JOB a fool for not admitting his mistake. The evidence was clear according to JOB's friends that there must have been some sin JOB was involved in that caused the destruction to take place. JOB's friends believe his sin was covered up by pride because of the statement JOB made that he was sinless.

JOB's friends spoke about the laws of God and how they operate. At the same time, these laws become accusations when applied to JOB in this situation. Yes, God's laws are what they are, but used while JOB is suffering, they lack compassion and imply JOB is wrong about his belief of blamelessness and comes off as an accusation. This type of thinking is in every religious or non-religious organization. Knowing the difference between being disciplined and Satan's attacks are something I will not go into here because I am not sure of the difference myself. It is something to think about because the line is not clear.

The strategy of Satan was to cause confusion and conflict within JOB's mind and heart. JOB knew he was innocent. When God's laws are retold to JOB, they were supposed to cause JOB to say to himself, "yes, I must be in sin that I am not aware of, otherwise, I would not have this trouble in my life." How many times are you absolutely sure about something and something comes along telling you the opposite. It causes confusion and conflict in the brain. Your belief systems are deeply challenged and then you do not know what to believe anymore.

My life is riddled with such confusion. One such incident of my past was so intense with conflict that it kept me from succeeding by changing my beliefs. My belief system was attacked at a very early age.

My father was an alcoholic which explains much of what happened and why. There were few times when I spoke to him where he was not feeling the affects of alcohol. I have forgiven him for not knowing what he was doing and the pain he inflicted upon himself and me. He would never admit he was an alcoholic. Unfortunately, I learned to participate in the partying when I was old enough to do so. Later, I stopped drinking to excess and moved to a social way of drinking. Finally, I gave it up all together for a couple of reasons. I found I felt depressed the next day after drinking, and on top of that, I wanted to play soccer until I am 75.

When I was young, my dad would give me mixed signals. One signal did a lot of damage to the point where I created a safe place to go inside because of the intensity. Some people are not so lucky and the wiring in the brain shorts out. My dad told us boys not to hit girls of which was mainly directed toward my younger sister because the four of us children would wrestle and fight all the time. And, needless to say, someone would always get hurt.

Well, one day my cousin Willie was going to fight a boy in the neighborhood for some dumb reason. I went out to watch because I never saw a real fight. Nothing happened for a long time so I turned around to go back home.

As I was walking back to my house, a boy with his sister stepped in front of me blocking my passage wanting to fight with me. I told the boy I was not interested. He said, "You will fight my sister then." I said no again. She hit me in the nose anyway knocking me down to the ground on my back and unconscious for a couple of seconds. I got up and she did it again. They walked away because they saw I was not going to fight.

My dad saw what had happened and proceeded to harass me for months afterwards about how I got beat up by a girl and was chicken to fight back. This confused me because I was told not to hit a girl, but he hammered and degraded me with some very harsh words. The pain of being beat down by a girl, the degrading from my dad, stories at school, and the disgrace I felt caused me to create a safe place inside of me that had no feelings whatsoever to deal with the confusion. I created an impenetrable wall.

Children do not know how to deal with this type of deep conflict, so they create a variety of responses, mentally or physically, to lessen the pain and confusion. I was lucky, I just created a place inside that was safe and removed any feelings at all. I became a brick wall where accusations would bounce right off. This later proved to be detrimental to my marriage until it was uncovered and dealt with.

As life unfolded, and my lack of social skills showed through other events of my life along with intense confusing situations on a consistent basis from my dad, I came to a belief that girls did not like me. I had contact with girls, but when they got to know me, they soon left.

Fortunately, God found me. I was not looking for him. I then studied the Bible. My life was transformed and my first girlfriend became my wife, whom I met at age 35. I received help from a family therapist named Todd Spath and now work on integrating the confusion inside.

The strength of character JOB had to make it through this first challenging attack was amazing. The conflicting message was intense. He did not sin but everything in his life pointed to it. JOB believed there was no sin worthy of the destruction that took place in his life. There may have been sin in his life, as there is with all of us, but the sin was not worthy of what happened.

JOB's character was such that he would give sacrifices for his children just because he thought they "may" have sinned. JOB was well aware of ensuring his sins and the sins of his children were atoned for through sacrifices. I wonder why JOB's friends did not catch that JOB had this kind of heart.

What do the expression of these laws look like today in the religious community? God's laws are for the benefit of humanity and Jesus came to "fulfill" the law. Believe it or not, most of us are similar to Eliphaz and his friends. We talk about God through expressing the "facts" about who God is and what he is about. We express the knowledge we have accumulated throughout the years from studying the Bible believing this is what people need or want to hear. When asked about our belief in God, most of us talk about what we know or how it has affected our lives. This is only part of the picture, only half of the whole. It is as if we are stuck in the Old Testament with all the facts about the New Testament.

Our responses are usually the same as Eliphaz and his friends when confronted with why we believe in the Bible or what the Bible has to offer. God is this. God is that. God is love. God is great, etc. When are we going to stop and pay attention to the other person and the suffering or confusion they are going through by not committing to living as God commands? What is it going to take to get us out of the religious mindset that God is a set of facts? Jesus came down to get us out of this 'law' mindset, but we migrate right back to the time when Israel was living in the desert learning about the laws and making sure to follow them.

I watched Bill Maher's TV show a few times, mainly because we do not have mainstream cable at our house. I had a chance to see a film by Bill Maher called "Religulous," which was very entertaining and eye opening. He goes on this search for why people believe what they believe about God. Of course, he adds his style of comedy to the film, which comes from the devil's advocate point of view – in opposition to the ideas expressed. However, he opened up some very interesting points not answerable by the people he confronted. He confronted Jewish, Christians, and Muslims from around the globe.

The most amazing part of the show to me was the response of the people he encountered. Some were educated and some were not. Some were in positions of power and others were not. He interviewed people from a wide variety of lifestyles. I was taken aback that the people he encountered all had the same thing to say – what they knew were the facts of the religion they followed. Not one offered any comfort to him on his journey to find the truth. Not one recognized Mr. Maher's needs or his inner desires. No one saw he was looking to find peace in knowing the truth. No one recognized what I believe is his pain of not knowing the truth of whether there is a god. Not one person related to Bill Maher. They only produced the facts about what they have studied and why these facts were true. Because we all can put our faith in facts, right? We can all put our faith in the law? God's laws are true, aren't they?

All we need to do is act like an answering machine and send out the message that was copied in to our machine of all the facts we have accumulated? Sure, why not, it is a lot easier than actually getting in touch with someone and how they are feeling. Not one person offered the position of finding the truth by coming to an understanding of seeing yourself before the cross so that God can reveal himself to that person. The most important part of committing to God is where God reveals himself. Facts do not do that. A sincere desire to know if God will reveal himself to someone is the destination.

Laws are for the guilty. The guilt trip is used extensively by people everywhere. The facts are there to make us feel guilty. "You did not take out the trash." "You did not make the bed." "Your grades are horrendous." "*I myself have seen a fool taking root, but suddenly his house was cursed.* (JOB)" You get the meaning. The accusations of guilt fly as Eliphaz and his friends try to make JOB admit his guilt.

To admit your guilt when you are not guilty breaks the foundation you once depended upon, which then vanishes in thin air. Where would you stand at that point? There is nothing to stand upon.

Countless people have been considered guilty of something they did not do. My children are classic examples of this assumption of guilt. One of their toys comes up missing quite often. The thief is always the other child. The blame game starts and the other child knows for sure the other one took it. I ask if they saw them take it. Were they there when the toy was taken – actually watching the other child take it? The answer is almost always "no." They were not there to watch them take it. I then ask why they are blaming the other child. It starts at an early age and continues through life.

The feeling of being guilty is one of the most powerful and damaging psychological characteristic anyone can experience. Feeling guilty for something channels people's lives and actions in a variety of directions. Guilt can be directed toward other people or ourselves. The movie Goodwill Hunting explained well this psychology of the mind. Robin Williams, who portrays a psychologist, coaches Matt Damon on his life and finally gets through to Matt Damon about him being innocent and not guilty of his past. Matt needed to know he was not guilty of the incidents of his past in order to move forward in his life.

JOB's Friends also had knowledge of the consequence of hidden sin. When someone hides sin, he or she tries really hard not to have the sin exposed. We deceive ourselves about the hidden sin and make up all kinds of lies to cover it up. These lies can include the deceptive false humility or a false openness to being taught or shown the truth. JOB's humility in asking to be shown where he went wrong would have been taken to believe he was falsely humble. He tells them they are speaking the truth and those truthful words are painful. JOB is in a desperate state while having boils all over his skin, and his friends are not listening to or believing what JOB says because of their belief about him being in sin. JOB describes to his friends that they treat his words as wind, having no solidity, or foundation from which to stand upon. They appear and then are gone.

I have had a very clear understanding about words being as wind because of hidden sin. My wife and I were helping a couple in their first year of marriage. We would get together at least once a week for counseling giving them a viewpoint from someone who was not involved emotionally in their relationship. Every meeting, there was some sort of issue that had to be resolved. Trust issues were at the heart of their marriage. They had a difficult time trusting each other. We would sit down and go over the issue of the week, find a solution to the issue, but there was no headway on deepening the trust between them. I resolved to believe that this issue of trust was going to take time to heal.

This was not the first couple we had helped with trust issues. Trust issues are apparent in every marriage. Trust is a decision. Decisions are based upon previous experiences and beliefs. Learning to trust takes time to develop which change the beliefs that hinder acceptance by the other person. Many people understand this and work hard in deciding to trust. Trust is a building block of any relationship and does not come automatically. Without trust, marriages will fail.

After a year of constant counseling, the couple split up and decided to get a divorce. We were shocked by their decision because we felt it just needed time. We were wrong, however, because what came out after that decision to separate was the real issue that had stopped the building of trust in that marriage. Un-confessed sin.

In the church I attend, mainly because it is a biblical command from God, it was commonplace for couples to wait to have any sexual contact, including kissing for some, until they were married. The couple, when they first met and became friends, had sexual relations, which was never confessed. This provided the basis for the removal of trust in the marriage since the command of God is clear. The atmosphere of the church was to refrain from this activity and confess if it happened. Not only was trust lost, but also the guilt of the act was a huge burden to them. If they had confessed the act, they could have received help to overcome their issue, as many have done and succeeded. Unfortunately, their confession was too late. This type of practice of not disclosing sin happened to more than a few people who suffered the consequences of divorce.

God commands people to get married first and then to have sexual relations. This provides the basis from which to build trust. Friendship develops instead of the physical relationship. If it is decided between the couple that the friendship is not strong enough to move toward a marriage, the friendship will stay just what it is, a friendship.

If the friendship turns to a deeper love for each other, the next steps are taken. Sometimes in the engagement stage, the relationship stops and returns to friendship, and since there is no physical relationship, people remain friends.

Once the relationship makes it to the final stage of marriage, the physical aspect of the relationship comes into play. People have not been hurt along the way, trust has been built to communicate a commitment to one another and that each person really cares about the other, a friendship has developed, and the final consummation of that friendship and love provides a great foundation for the best chance of surviving the disasters of life. And, from my standpoint, the anticipation was overwhelming for my sacred day of marriage.

JOB's friends assumed that JOB was lying and hiding sin because God's laws are powerful and true. The consequences of not following God's laws were evident in those days in a variety of ways. Everyone knew following the law was of utmost importance. Following the laws became so important that it overshadowed the real intent of the law in the first place.

I am not so sure if I were one of JOB's friends that I would have done anything different. Given the fact that there was the added thrust from Satan himself would make it more difficult to do anything different.

At the end of the chapter, God only says JOB's friends are in the wrong and to offer the appropriate sacrifices for them. If JOB's friends were completely out of line, God would have been angered by them, as he was with a number of people in the Old Testament, and probably dealt with them as he did with those who lacked faith by building a calf of gold, complained of no food after coming through the Red Sea, etc. God knew that JOB's friends were partly right and uses the story of JOB to teach us about what types of weapons are used by Satan. Being shot at by the weapon of God's laws hurts.

For years and years, JOB's friends showed trust in JOB's decisions, his lifestyle, his integrity, and his love for his friends. He did not lie to them. How could they now determine that JOB was lying to their face? Why could they not believe JOB's statements? One scripture in Psalms 36:2 describes the essence of blind pride.

Psalms 36:2 In their own eyes they flatter themselves too much to detect or hate their sin.

Pride is something that cannot be detected by the person that is prideful because the person is too busy flattering himself or herself. The person is incapable of understanding his or her situation no matter what is involved. That means someone else having an objective view or understanding of the situation or circumstance must point out to the prideful person the inherent lack of knowing or understanding they are being prideful.

JOB states his innocence, but the situation or circumstance points to a different understanding by JOB's friends. Children are a classic example of this phenomenon and one of the funniest situations captured on video displayed on America's Funniest Home Videos with frequency.

A child has taken a magic marker or a similar coloring tool and has written all over their face, furniture, walls, or floors. When asked by the parent if they had done anything wrong, the child confidently says "no" as the evidence points to a different answer. The child's very confidence lacks the connection with the activity that just took place and the actual meaning of the situation. We are not above this type of pride. As we get older, when our beliefs are challenged, most of us do not like to be wrong about what we know to be true. I will say it certainly is difficult to have someone point out our pride.

Understanding Pride is something we cannot see in ourselves, we should seek out people we can trust to help us identify our pride. However, exposing our pride hits deep in our soul and is a painful experience for all of us. So, many of us take on a false humility so we do not feel the pain from our pride being exposed.

Pride is the main diet of humanity though. Sometimes pride is very destructive and other times it is funny. I will give you a personal example I find to be very comical. My family has a particular pride I have come to understand. I am sure we are not unique and that others suffer from this particular type of pride as well. My friends have pointed this pride out, and I have acknowledged I have it. I have a difficult time controlling it too.

From the history with my family, we tend to know everything about everything and can confidently speak about issues we know nothing about.

I did this experiment with my family, as well as other people, that proved to me this false sense of knowing about everything. I would start a conversation with my family or people and ask them if they knew about a topic such as cold fusion, or something they would know nothing about. They would express their deep knowledge of the subject, and I would interject with small facts about the subject.

All of a sudden, the individual I am speaking with would completely know those facts I just interjected. However, the facts I interjected were not true statements or facts.

This is a common occurrence in our society. We all want to be considered as intelligent and knowledgeable. We cultivate the attitude of 'Keeping up with the Jones' more or less known as pride.

Trying to differentiate between what is fact and fiction is a difficult process. Admitting we are wrong helps our beliefs change and accept new true information we come across that is contradictory to our own beliefs and truths. A majority of us do not want to be wrong on any account.

Those who are open to being wrong are the ones that are more apt to have their beliefs changed, knowledge expanded, and truth exposed. I have to admit I will send my cousin Gary certain information thinking I am in the right. He sends back an email telling me I am completely uninformed and unknowledgeable about the issue. I respect his knowledge because of his education. It is hard to be humbled by him often. I have to remind him that he lived with me for two years and that is where he gained most of his knowledge. I do not think he believes that though.

I would confidently assume that JOB's friends were well aware of pride that infiltrates our souls. They must have studied Psalms and Proverbs to help identify, become knowledgeable, and prepared in order to deal with pride. Proverbs says a multitude of times, "God hates pride."

JOB's friends were overly confident in their assessment of the situation. I believe this was partly due to the dark figure that came in Eliphaz's sleep, which confirmed the knowledge of God's laws and experiences with people through life.

I am not above this type of thinking either. I have caught myself in several situations where I was sure of the situation and circumstances only to be wrong about everything. It is a humbling experience to be wrong. This humbling experience has helped me to become more aware of how I respond to situations and circumstances. Rather than be quick to assess the situation and make a decision based upon what I know and understand, I have tried to become more inquisitive. This type of thinking has proven to be effective in reducing the number of humbling situations I am involved. Nevertheless, like all people, I am human and humbling is a good thing after-the-fact. During the humbling experience, I am not overjoyed to say the least.

We need to understand God's laws can be used as a weapon, a snare, and a blessing. Understanding JOB's story and the weapons that were used on him will help us in our walk. Using God's laws as a weapon to break someone's belief can be damaging beyond repair. Treading lightly on legal issues with a humble heart, together with an understanding of not always knowing the truth, even when we believe deeply with all of our heart, soul, and mind, makes us rely on God more – just where God wants us to be.

The Character Weapon

The next step taken by Satan after hitting JOB with the concept of God's laws is to use the character of God. Reinforcing God's character helps us to understand what we are not as opposed to who God is. JOB's friends do not accept that JOB already knows God's character because their pride blinds them from understanding. So, they express the facts of God's character. God does not pervert justice. God is trustworthy, patient, merciful, honest, has integrity, always right, and there is nothing wrong with any of God's decisions; you get the point. The use of God's character as a solid trustworthy source to stand upon is being used as a weapon to try to make JOB submit in reverence, even if JOB is in the right.

Many people have a belief that just knowing there is a God is enough however untrue that may be. That would be the same thing as knowing there is a car parked in my driveway that can take me anywhere I want, but never getting in. I know it is there, and I can drive it when I want. I just never get in to go anywhere.

How many friends would any of us have if we just knew our friend Bob was there but did not know anything about him? How deep would the relationship be? How would we know who they are? Their likes? Their dislikes? What makes them happy? What makes them sad? What are the things they do not like us to do? What do they expect from us in order to have a relationship? How many of us would have friends if we continued to be mean or not talk to them? None of us – to answer that question.

This is what confuses me about the Jewish religion. They have a belief that one cannot say God's name. The relationship between man and God does not exist. Man is only to obey what is written. JOB's friends believe they cannot challenge God in absolutely anything as expressed in JOB 37:19 *"Tell us what we should say to him; we cannot draw up our case because of our darkness. Should he be told that I want to speak? Would anyone ask to be swallowed up?"* And, JOB 37:23 *"The Almighty is beyond our reach..."* However, God communicated to a multitude of people over the 1500 years of the Old Testament, including JOB. We call this a relationship. In one man's relationship, he asked for help from God and God obliged. *"The sun stopped in the middle of the sky and delayed going down about a full day. There has never been a day like it before or since, a day when the LORD listened to a human being."* (Joshua 10:13-14) Joshua knew God's character and could rely upon it. Why is the relationship between God and man broken in the Jewish religion? There is no evidence in the old testament that states a man should not have a relationship with God – talk to him – ask him for answers – confess misdoings – say sorry – cry to – etc. In the Psalms, David cried to God.

      Why wouldn't God want a relationship with people? That is the reason why he created us was to have a relationship. He has a relationship with the angels, including Satan. He even asks Satan about his day in JOB 1. God says, "What's going on? Where have you come from?" Satan answers, "From throughout the earth going back and forth on it."

      God wanted to know where Adam and Eve were hiding. God spoke through a bush to Moses. God has written multitudes of conversations between himself and people in the Old Testament and in the New Testament. We are made in his image and we understand relationships. God understands relationships too. I do the same thing with my children when they come home from school. How was school? What did you do today? I am interested in them and the things they do. My relationship with our children is as important as my relationship with God.

The importance of realizing you can communicate with God can only be understated. I could not write the words to state how important it is to cultivate a relationship with God. God has never said to people that we should not communicate with him in either the Old Testament or the New Testament. There are countless examples throughout the Old Testament where God explains to his prophets (the people he communicates specifically to advance his purpose) that he has heard the prayers of those who were not prophets. Sometimes he answers those prayers through the prophets and sometimes he does not. God never said non-prophet people could not talk to him – not ever. Prophets are not the only people who can communicate with God.

As you come into a relationship with anyone, character becomes the most important aspect of knowing that person. Whenever I go to seminars, the speaker always talks about someone's character and how they live their life. They also express their own character through whatever area they acknowledge to be professionals.

Justifying character is as important in life as it is in the relationship with God. While in court, the defense is allowed to talk about the character of the person convicted of a crime before and after a guilty verdict. Lawyers are given the task to gather evidence on the character of the guilty party in order to receive a lesser penalty for the offense.

Governmental elections also characterize the individuals running for the position. The qualities the people running for office are expressed and are supposedly engrained in their character. By electing this person, we can expect this type of character to come forth. Unfortunately for politics, rarely does the character of the person come out to be true.

If we have an understanding about God, we know that his character is solid. We believe certain aspects of God's character to be absolute and can be completely relied upon. This provides a safe and secure relationship, one in which the boundaries are set, can be relied upon for support and knowledge, as well as peace in knowing, "I am in with the big guy and he is taking care of me." Comfort in knowing the solid foundation upon which the relationship is built is powerful and brings a sense of confidence for the individual who knows God's character to be solid as a rock.

We are fooled by people many times because the character we thought they had was hidden from us. Our mistakes can be attributed to our own beliefs. I tend to think people are honest because I am honest. I look for people who are honest. I sometimes am blinded by my own desire to see certain characteristics in people that are not there.

When I was in the Marine Corps, I was sent to a new duty station. I walked into the room I was assigned to and met my new roommate. He seemed like a nice guy. I went in to take a shower and came out only to realize he had stolen $160 from me. He had reached into my wallet when I was in the shower. I had just counted the money in the car before I came into the room, so I knew I had $160. Something told me to check when I got out of the shower. He lied about taking the money. I called the military police and finally received $140 back a couple of days later. He used the other $20 for a haircut. That was a big misjudgment on my part because I trusted him to be honest.

The relationships between men and women should be built upon the understanding we have a sinful nature. If we do not have this understanding, the relationship will fail. The other's sin is hurtful to us and our sin is hurtful to them. This creates a lack peace, comfort, and confidence in the relationship that needs help.

Our relationships are push and pull with no solid foundation from which to stand firm except for the foundation God provides to help us. People put up defenses and walls to protect themselves from being hurt. On top of that, our beliefs change on a consistent basis about the relationship through circumstances that present themselves. This becomes a constant battle to remain trusting and honest with each other.

God's character is what everyone's character should be like. If everyone was like God, we could completely rely on each other's character. When this belief about God's character is challenged in us, we are susceptible to wavering and changing beliefs that can be very damaging. If we cannot rely upon God to be a solid rock for us, our beliefs crack and are destroyed – the very thing Satan wants for our life.

Once our belief is broken about the reliability of God, we are susceptible to believing anything that comes along – a blowing of the wind. (Ephesians 4:14) We come to an understanding that there is nothing in life solid enough to believe in if our beliefs about God are broken.

God is not unreliable. A few of the most important concepts expressed by JOB's friends about God's reliable character are:

Does God pervert Justice?
Does the Almighty pervert what is right?
Surely, God does not reject one who is blameless or strengthen the hands of evildoers.
God has forgotten some of your sin.
God's wisdom is higher than the heavens, deeper than the depths, measure longer than the earth, and wider than the sea.
God recognizes deceivers and takes note of evil.

JOB's friends tried to use the truth about God's character as a weapon because God is absolutely right and reliable. JOB's belief about God would have been broken to shreds if not for the strength of JOB. JOB knew there was something wrong about the situation. God punished someone while there was no sin in his life to be punished for. If JOB believed the lie, then God cannot be relied upon. God is not what God says he is. You can see the pattern of thinking JOB would go down, which would completely destroy any faith, belief, trust, love, or hope in God. This is the ploy of Satan. Satan wants us to be destroyed in our thoughts about God.

In Satan's efforts to break JOB, because JOB was right and had not sinned, Satan uses God's character as a weapon through JOB's friends to try to break JOB's belief about being clean from sin.

Using someone's character to get a person to do something is inherent in our society. Manipulation is a common theme in JOB too. You see it in movies, the playground, the workplace, and even in marriages. The movies are a classic example of using character to get a specific response from someone.

The scene unfolds with the mobster boss standing over one of his own men wanting his servant to do something. The mobster boss explains he or she had better do what is asked or you know how Vinny (the torturer) likes to take care of people. The character of Vinny enjoys tearing people from limb to limb. The mobster boss uses Vinny's character as a weapon to make people do what is expected.

I have used God's character as a weapon when studying the Bible with people. I realize when the person I study with understand God's character, it is usually enough to move a person to come to terms with the idea they are nothing without God. However, I find myself stepping in trying to spear his or her heart into submission rather than allowing God to do the work. I am no different from JOB's friends. The spirit of Satan is leading me when I am brandishing my Bible weapon. I have not laid down my weapon completely and turned it into a plowshare yet. *"They shall beat their swords into plowshares, and their spears into pruning-hooks: nation shall not lift up sword against nation, neither shall they learn war any more."* (Isaiah 2:4)

The reason it is so easy to use God's character as a weapon is that no one escapes God's wrath. Everyone is under the laws of God. Still, multitudes of people do not believe this. Excuses are as infinite as the stars in the sky. I have heard probably half of that sky while studying with people. But Romans 1:20 says *"For since the creation of the world God's invisible qualities—his eternal power and divine nature—have been clearly seen, being understood from what has been made, so that people are without excuse."* Eliphaz states this concept to JOB too, He will not escape the darkness; a flame will wither his shoots, and the breath of God's mouth will carry him away. Let him not deceive himself by trusting what is worthless, for he will get nothing in return. (JOB 15:30-31)

On the flipside of the concept of using God's character as a weapon is the concept of 2 Corinthians 6:7 *"...in truthful speech and in the power of God; with weapons of righteousness in the right hand and in the left..."* and 2 Corinthians 10:4 *"The weapons we fight with are not the weapons of the world."* are two scriptures expressing weapons to be used.

What are the weapons we use? How do we use them? Well, if we look at the scripture, "truthful speech," "God," and "righteousness" are our weapons. I do not see love in amongst those weapons. I am not saying love is bad, just not used as a weapon for God. I would venture to say that righteousness tops the list and encompasses the other parts. If love were important, JOB would have been commended for his love. As you know, he sacrificed for his children and loved to follow the laws of God.

We, as Christians, will try to use love as a weapon to bring people into a relationship with God. We love these people with an overwhelming love and commitment until they become Christians. Then we back off our love, and sometimes to the point of having very little contact with them after they commit to God. What does that tell them? We are no different from those who are not Christians. I have seen very little positives from this type of weapon. The Bible says we must continue to teach them. (Matt 28:18-20)

Using compassion created by love along with truthful speech and obedience to the principles of the Bible and desire to be righteousness is our light. Righteousness then shines like a light that pierces the darkness in our hearts bringing peace to our souls, not firearms and grenades.

The weapon of truthful speech combined with righteousness learned from God is the most powerful weapon in the world. A person cannot have truthful speech without righteousness and visa versa. They go hand in hand. If all I had was love and no righteousness, then I am a clanging cymbal. If all I had was righteousness and no love, I am the same.

When Jesus saved Mary, the prostitute, he did not say, "Go, I love you." He told her to leave her life of sin – become righteous. He did not tell Zacheus, "I just want you to know I love you." He told Zacchaeus, "Today, salvation has come to this house." This is because Zacchaeus wanted to be righteous. There is a difference between thinking and believing in God and living a righteous life. God's love is supposed to propel us into living righteously.

How can I tell people the truth if I do not live it myself? This is where the power comes in. It is difficult to live the truth through righteousness. This is why Paul boasted in his shortcomings or weaknesses. Righteousness comes from confessing and repenting from sin. Because this is such a difficult task, we need to kneel down before God begging for strength to do so.

I have been down on my knees so many times; I am surprised I do not have calluses all over them. God called me when I was 32 years old. I had to do some growing up for the next three years because I was so messed up mentally and heartfully. By the time I was 34, I was distraught because I was not married yet and had no girlfriend. For some reason, the number 34 made me feel old.

I used to do acting and modeling in Hollywood, so somehow I was considered photogenic. I was so messed up mentally that my friends in the church used to say I had the "sin of weirdness." They could not put a description on me other than that. I later realized I could not understand what a relationship was. My lack of knowledge of what a relationship was defined by my "sin of weirdness."

In addition, because of the damage throughout my life, I was completely afraid to express my true feelings. Because I had the sin of weirdness that told me I was not like Jesus, I felt inadequate and different from others. There was no one like me as far as I thought because the weapon used against me was used to separate me from others.

I decided to go out to the park once a week and cry out to God. I chose to walk to a nearby park around 10:00pm. I would stay there for about an hour praying with all my heart. I knew there would be few, if any, people there to make me feel embarrassed as I poured out my soul to God. I talked to God for one reason. That reason was to come to a peace in my heart that I was going to be alone for the rest of my life. I was trying to be at peace with being single and not married.

I cried many tears of sadness and pain. I came to the truth during those times I was just a lump of flesh with sin on it incapable of being righteous. I talked to God about not being a person God could trust with a Christian sister. I was completely inadequate to take care of a Christian sister and be a provider, a faithful support for her, and a righteous rock she could lean on. I severely lacked the tools to have a relationship. Six months later after crying in the park once or twice a week, my heart was transformed somehow. I was at peace with living single for the rest of my life. Funny thing is

I then met my wife. She is the strongest person I know because I put her through some difficult times while learning to have a relationship with her.

The truth is my friends in the church kept speaking the truth in love to me. They were right about my sin of weirdness. I had a weird pride too. The pride of being an actor and model told me I was awesome and should have several women wanting me. Yes, it was conflicting and confusing. The experiences in my life compounded my weirdness to tell me women did not like me.

Coming to the grips with my poor character helped me to humble out and realize I was not worthy of a woman. This was the key that made the difference. If God were to give me a woman to marry, I was not worthy to have her. This is different from me believing I am capable or awesome enough to have a woman. I needed to realize if God were to give me a woman, she would be a prize possession to be valued, cherished, loved, and sacrificed for. No wonder I was so messed up. I was trying to get them to love someone who believed he was unlovable. I realized I was not worthy of Jesus during those times either. I was not worthy of his sacrifice for me in order to know God.

The truth in love my friends spoke to me would not have been powerful unless they were trying to be righteous themselves. We have been on our knees together crying to God about our sin and the desire to repent from it many times. My friends desire to be righteous was contagious. The more we tried to be righteous because of the love of Jesus, the more our hearts were exposed and sin dealt with, repented from, and freedom from sin emerged in our lives. We were being unchained from the world of darkness. Our love for each other increased. Our love for God increased. We started seeing the fruit of our righteousness and the deepening love for God. Because of the truth, we were being set free.

John 8:31-32 *"To the Jews who had believed him, Jesus said, "If you hold to my teaching, you are really my disciples. Then you will know the truth, and the truth will set you free."* We had to be disciples disciplined in righteousness to speak the truth in order to be set free. Jesus provided the pathway to understanding God loved us enough to teach us righteousness and truth. Until Jesus died on a cross, only Jews had the chance at righteousness, truth, and faith.

Unfortunately, we as humans will use truth and righteous as a weapon for selfish means. Righteousness and truth can be used as a form of control, a way to make people believe the way you want them to, and a whole variety of other sins. Of course, this is done under the disguise of truth and righteousness. It is not really truth and righteousness.

This is the reason why studying the Bible ourselves, testing the spirits, testing what we know with other people who study the Bible, and compiling the knowledge into wisdom is so important. We need to be careful though because, Oooooh boy, do we like to be knowledgeable and wise, which becomes pride.

I have encountered the "wisdom" and "knowledge" of people given to others that has been completely out of line with their life. This is why we are to seek advice from many. One of my friends had been dating a woman online for about two years. She lived in another country and was not able to visit him, or him to her, very often. He was over the age of 30 and so was she.

He was known to have some very unusual personality and character issues. He received some advice from people, which could have been very damaging. They told him to wait to be engaged that he needed more time to work on his character. His character was used as a weapon to stop him from moving forward in the relationship. His character was not like Jesus; therefore, he needed to wait. I asked if they knew anything about his experience with the woman or his life. My friend said they had not asked about the relationship and only knew of his character.

If my friend had taken that advice, the woman would have gotten tired of waiting for a husband, because she was not young, and more than likely sought someone who was more committed to going all the way into marriage. If he had waited, he would have looked like he was scared of commitment. I told him the advice he received could be very damaging and was not the truth.

The truth about the situation was found in a question I presented to him, "did he love her enough to be fully committed to her for the rest of his life?" They had enough time to get to know each other. They were older and not young and immature. He had to ask his own heart whether he wanted to live with her for the rest of his life. His unusual character and personality traits would be challenged through his commitment to the marriage.

Marriage challenges and changes our character and personality. We need to be sure we are going to be totally committed to going through any circumstance or situation, because two sinners coming together, sacrificing themselves to the relationship at all costs, even to the point of possibly denying God because of the relationship, is not easy to sustain or handle. Obviously, the multitudes of rewards are to be considered too. My friend prayed and realized this was the one for him. I told him to move forward, which he did and has been happily married, not without its challenges though.

How much value and truth would I have given to my friend if I had not wanted to be righteous and truthful myself? My words would have been like a hot air balloon floating with no solid foundation from which to stand upon. I loved my friend, but I loved him with truth and righteousness. I loved my friend so much I desired to have him know the truth and call him to righteousness too. He does the same for me.

His character traits are still humorous, which makes him who he is.

Using God's character as a weapon is something we all do at times. Our pride of having knowledge and wisdom and the desire to see people come into a relationship with God can turn into weapons of mass destruction, especially if our own desire for righteousness and truth are lacking.

JOB withstood the attacks from Satan with amazing strength of character. In order for us to withstand the attacks from Satan, we need to seek truth and righteousness in our own life. The truth was JOB did not sin. His desire for righteousness enabled him to question his situation with God and ask for clarification. God is truly more than a god, he is a god who is not above approach. We can confidently approach God in every situation or circumstance, which allows us to deflect the weaponry used to break us to pieces.

Twister

"A superior man in dealing with the world is not for anything or against anything. He follows righteousness as the standard." — Confucius

The game of Twister is a fun game. A mat with different colored dots lies on the floor while someone spins a spinner that lands on a color and the people playing the game have to touch that color. Everyone is twisted up as he or she tries to touch the color. The game goes on until individuals fall down and one is left to win the game.

Such is the game of communication between people. Words are communicated, emotions flare, and the messages are twisted up until one or both fall. Unlike the game of Twister, people are usually hurt by the fall. Afterward, beliefs change, and many times couples or friends separate.

Twisting words for our benefit is called manipulation. We have seen this type of scene in movies where a not so bright individual is coerced by a bad guy to do something he or she does not want to do. As the not so bright individual is speaking, the bad guy turns the words around on them. The not so bright individual ends up believing he or she actually said the twisted words themselves. Eventually, what they originally did not want to do, they end up doing because they believe they came up with the thought themselves.

The laws of God, the character of God, have been used to assault JOB, and now Satan assaults JOB's words. So far, Satan has been losing the battle to break JOB. He has to go for the jugular – a last ditch chance to break JOB. There is nothing left for Satan to assault. Satan has covered all his bases by destroying his family, his animals, his physical well-being, made his wife turn against him, hammered in the laws of God, and tried to spear him with the character of God.

We know that righteous character often weakens in the face of trials. Enron is proof is this concept because I am sure Kenneth Lay did not set out to commit fraud. Through trials of the character, he weakened and allowed sin to live within himself and the organization. We all allow sin to peak its head up in our lives at times though.

JOB's friends take the words of JOB and twist them to create the meaning they want. Satan used this method in the Garden of Eden. "Now the serpent was more crafty than any of the wild animals the LORD God had made. He said to the woman, 'Did God really say, you must not eat from any tree in the garden'?" (Gen 3:1) Satan started with a question and ended with the statement, "'*You will not certainly die*,' the serpent said to the woman. (Gen 3:4) In attacking JOB's character, Satan must find a way to make JOB believe JOB was the one who spoke the twisted statements made by JOB's friends. This in turn will raise his emotional state to weaken his mind and heart.

My wife and I get into battles of who said what and when as we try to work through a situation. The more we claim what was right and who was wrong, the higher the emotional state would rise between us. At times, the argument would escalate to the point where neither of us is talking to the other.

These battle of words cause great emotional stress and there are some instances where the decisions made during these times were not spiritual ones. We were NOT drawn together by our actions, but driven apart. I have had to get into the car and drive somewhere to cool down at times. My thoughts would entertain going into unthinkable sin, and I have come close. The intensity of the emotions would sometimes carry over into the next day because the battle escalated to Jupiter.

These times of being separated cause the mind and heart to have a wide range of emotional energy. In this emotional state, rash decisions can be made about a variety of things, including damaging our beliefs. We can decide to believe we should not be married or blame God and believe God is not on our side.

Satan tries to twist the emotional knife into JOB's heart to escalate his emotional state in an effort to have JOB make rash decisions or entertain Godless thoughts.

Our emotions are the catalyst to many bad decisions. Companies know this and advertise in a way to cause people to purchase products emotionally and impulsively. The consumerist attitude has been driven into our society at all levels. People are deceived in believing the money for the product does not matter – that having the product matters more. They want the product at all costs whether or not they need it. Advertisers have meddled their way into football turning a 60-minute game with 11 minutes of actual playtime into a two and a half hour barrage of advertisements. The sad thing is we accept this.

The advertised product fills an emotional need in people in order to get them to want the product. I feel the battle to purchase impulsively in the area of food and groceries, which is weird for a man. We have taken action against this by setting budgetary guidelines. We give ourselves a certain amount of cash to purchase food for the month, and when it runs out, we must be creative to eat. This causes my wife and I to think about whether or not what we are purchasing is necessary. Our food bills have dropped drastically and our health in eating has increased dramatically. However, the conviction waivers at times. I do not believe God wants us to live this way, wavering to and fro.

As a society, if we practice impulsive purchasing on a consistent basis, we will end up in the poor house and in debt. Companies need money to flow and work very hard to keep compulsiveness alive and well.

The emotions behind compulsive purchasing are addicting and habitual in nature. I do not need to prove anything here because alcohol such as beer and wine addictions prove the entire mindset. The emotions attached to alcohol caused by advertising have become a well-oiled machine to ensure they continue. Advertisers make us believe football without alcohol is depressing and with it, is exciting.

JOB's friends do a good job of heightening JOB's emotional state. JOB fires back at Zophar in JOB 12:1 *"Doubtless you are the people, and wisdom will die with you."* JOB is now embroiled in sarcasm against his harsh friends. JOB defends his knowledge of God, *"what you know, I know"* JOB has taken a defensive posture to fight the barrage of attacks of his friends on his character. He goes so far as to call them liars. JOB's emotional state becomes highly combative. The lack of compassion, the assaults by the laws and character of God, and the non-belief that JOB is telling the truth are getting to JOB.

JOB's friends believe JOB is wrong and being prideful. Proverbs talks a lot about pride and the blindness that stems from pride. Pride develops in our soul. The only way out is for someone to come and point out the pride. Satan tries to use JOB's statement *"...I am blameless..."* (JOB 9:21) and twist it to claim absolute purity or having no sin at all. Satan attacks JOB's words by twisting them hoping to convince JOB of his pride before God.

One of the scriptures I like the most in the book of JOB is *"Though the pride of the godless person reaches to the heavens and his head touches the clouds, he will perish forever, like his own dung"* (JOB 20:6) JOB's friends are trying to make JOB realize he is like dung if he keeps being prideful. However, JOB already knows he is just the dust of the earth that has come to life.

I heard it said years ago that if we were reduced to our elements, we were only 97 cents worth of minerals. With inflation, we are probably about $2 to $5 now. We are just lumps of flesh with sin and those that are baptized, have the Holy Spirit. The Holy Spirit lives in lumps of flesh with sin. Comforting! God purchased our lumps of flesh worth $2 with the life of Jesus. Starbucks coffee is worth more than we are. But, we understand as Christians that we are valued because of the death of Jesus.

JOB's character and reputation had been reduced to that of an earthworm when all these things happened to him. Nothing from the past entered into the minds of JOB's friends. They were convinced that JOB's character had changed. He had no integrity. He was full of pride. He was blinded by his arrogance. He had fallen into the trap of sin that snared him and took him down. JOB's friends believe God has charged JOB with wrongdoing and try to get through to JOB, "*Is it for your piety that he rebukes you and brings charges against you? Is not your wickedness great? Are not your sins endless?*" (JOB 22:4-5)

When I became a Christian and committed to following the Bible and God, my character changed dramatically. I was so different from the way I was before, my family thought I was part of a religious cult. I did not find this out for a couple of years after I was baptized. I used to drink and cuss, speak sarcasms, put people down, and a whole variety of other damaging actions before being a Christian. My character changed, my mind changed, and my heart changed.

I would speak of the things God was doing for me, how great I felt, the experience I went through while becoming a Christian when he revealed himself to me, and the incredible friends I now have. I was happy and free and wanted my family to feel the same.

I considered integrity and righteousness to be of the utmost importance, to learn it, to live it, and to speak it. My character was different. My family saw the changes and did what I did growing up – found fault with the change, clung on to fear, and talked behind my back.

My grandmother, before she died, told me how they felt and what they spoke of. I was shocked. My own family, the ones who supposedly accepted me for who I am, had persecuted me. I had changed, but JOB had seemingly changed too according to his friends.

I had learned to fear God. JOB feared God. JOB's friends feared God. My family feared nothing. I, at one time, feared nothing too. To fear God is to realize the need to be obedient to what God commands. Just believing in God does not produce obedience. It takes a step of faith to be obedient. Fear is necessary for obedience. Proverbs says that the fear of God is the beginning of knowledge, and knowledge leads to wisdom. The proverb does not say, "To believe is the beginning of knowledge."

JOB's confidence in JOB 33:9 *"I am pure, I have done no wrong; I am clean and free from sin..."* must have shocked his friends. JOB was constantly aware of his sin and the sin of his children though. To make a statement such as this, in normal ways of thinking, would mean the person must have ceased to fear God or even be as pure as God.

Ceasing to fear God can be equated to pride because we are all with sin. Then, to go as far as desiring vindication from God because JOB had not sinned in order to cause the destruction is unbelievable. Before all this devastation happened, he knew he had sin, but had atoned for it. After the devastation, he believed he was not in sin. This would make JOB to have seemingly changed. I would have thought the same thing about JOB. One minute he is atoning for sin and the next he believes he did not sin. He was saying he did not sin to the point of having destruction brought upon him.

JOB's friends stay on track with trying to twist the meanings of JOB's words. A classic example I have used with people is in JOB 35:2, *"Do you think this is just? You say, 'I am in the right, not God.'"* Just about every time I have used this concept while studying with people, it has been the truth. When JOB's friends use it, they are trying to have JOB see the ridiculousness of JOB's thinking by equating JOB's feeling of being right while God is wrong. God cannot be wrong, ever.

Wars are fought between two sets of people who are certain they are right. I have often thought God has been wrong about my life. I am not alone in this. Just about everybody I know, who tries to live out the Bible, feels this way at times. We cannot see what God is doing for our lives. It is funny because we sometimes believe we know better than God does. He is all-knowing and he can see to the depths of our hearts. We are not all knowing and our hearts are deceitful. He can see the best path for us. However, this is difficult to accept.

After being a Christian for a few years, I started asking myself what my strength was and which job I should do. I came across a book with a test called "Discover What You Are Best At" by Linda Gayle and discovered I had an emotional negative feeling toward real estate. I challenged that thought and realized I had a deep love for it. I found a job in property management and excelled. God new what I needed by exposing me to the book.

The positive from that experience started me on the path to a college education. I did not decide to go to college. I was shoved into a corner and the only path out of the corner was to go to college. God decided I needed to go to college. I had opened myself up to asking God what is the best path, and to pin me down to travel on it.

While in college, I started realizing my heart had wanted to go to college all along but had deceived myself. I finally realized that God had a better plan. If I just listen to God and his signs in my life, I would be better off. My heart would be satisfied on a deep level. Moreover, this book came from listening to what God wanted me to do instead of me thinking better; and a little push from God too. It has been a challenging time though. My confidence in writing the book had to be placed with God and his guidance. I did not have JOB's confidence.

JOB expresses to his friends that he is willing to "*...take my life in my hands...*" (JOB 13:14) JOB follows up with "*I will surely defend my ways to his face. Indeed, this will turn out for my deliverance, for no godless man would dare come before him.*" JOB is stating confidently, forcefully, and aggressively to his friends in a heightened emotional state. The absolute conviction of JOB is astounding. To stand before God and claim his blamelessness, even at the expense of his own life - should have been enough for his friends to believe JOB. Satan's attack has heightened JOB's emotional state, but also heightened his conviction of his blamelessness before God.

JOB asks for compassion, love, loyalty, and friendship from his friends. JOB's friends were charged with getting JOB to admit his wrongdoing, which is exactly what Satan planned. If this were to happen, JOB's character of righteousness and faith would weaken and possibly die completely. This is probably the only time Satan had hope of something happening. We do not normally think of Satan having hope in anything, but I am sure he does.

Hebrews 11:1-2 says, "*Now faith is confidence in what we hope for and assurance about what we do not see.*" Remaining faithful is a difficult task. We are to have faith in the invisible, faith in the story of a man called Jesus, faith that God exists and wants to prosper us, love us, shape us, and be guidance for our life.

What happens when bad things happen to us? If God were good, why would he allow bad things to happen to us? This question comes to mind in every one of us when our faith weakens. The decisions we make during those times project us in a direction either toward God or away. Tragically, many make decisions away from God. Granted, suffering is difficult to understand, and as God says at the end of JOB, "I am God, did you create anything?" gives us no consolation.

We want freedom from suffering, but God says we are not free. Freedom vanishes with powerlessness, as we live through suffering. We must do what God expects and suffer what God dictates whether good or bad because he is God.

God is challenging our beliefs to create a righteous character. The belief that God is working for our good or bad, prosperity or demise, is for his purpose and is a core belief that needs strengthening. This strengthening is not only for our good, but also for others to see in our lives. Satan attacks our character and our character needs strengthening.

There are several examples in the Bible where innocent individuals were subjected to harsh experiences only to end in others around them accepting the God of the Israelites and subjecting themselves to God's way of life. I wonder whom JOB affected in this way.

Daniel is one prophet who experienced harsh treatment several times for his devotion to God. In Daniel 5, Daniel is subjected to sleeping in a lions den for a night. The king admired Daniel a great deal and was hoping his God would save him from the lions. When the king arrived at the den in the morning, the lions did not hurt Daniel because an angel had protected him. Afterward, the king proclaimed that everyone should worship the God that Daniel worships.

During the times of testing, God is trying to use our lives as examples to affect others around us to commit their lives to him. Believing in God's heart during our pain does not always happen though.

Our character is refined through suffering. I have not seen anyone's character change because of an incredible party and good times. They just want more parties and good times. Many times the pain is unbearable and confusing, which causes us to make decisions about our faith in the opposite direction of God. Satan also knows that the loss of faith of one affects others. Suffering is not to make us love more, but to grow our character and trust in the unseen.

How difficult was it for JOB to remain righteous and have faith even through the loss of his family, loss of everything he had, was inflicted with intense physical suffering, and the massive assault on his belief system by his trusted friends? This man is a hero in my book. It is no wonder God considered him a powerfully righteous and faithful man Satan himself could not break down. JOB was tested and he passed the test.

Movies with a similar concept are usually worth watching. Braveheart, and of course, The Passion of the Christ stand out among them all not because I like Mel Gibson, but because of the message contained in the movies.

So, Satan is trying to break our character strengths. God is allowing us to suffer to grow our character and strengthen our faith. Two opposing forces causing us to make decisions toward righteousness or not. We will be tested if we walk with God. There is no way out of this.

Why is it then churches teach we need to love each other more? Why is love on the forefront of every teaching? Granted love is necessary and the most important of all the teachings of God. Where are the teachings about righteousness? The prophets made it to heaven through righteousness and faith and not the love of Jesus. Jesus is the doorway for all of us to be able to understand what love is, not the end all be all if we JUST love. Having love does not make a person practice righteousness or faith either.

I have a friend who owns a business with another person. My friend grew up catholic and his business partner claimed to be a Christian. Events took place to expose the embezzlement of my friend's business partner. The business partner is a loving person, but his righteousness is lacking. For the business partner to take advantage of my friend is catastrophic to the friendship they had. Trust was destroyed. Guilt was deployed. The example of Jesus, who is also the example of righteousness, was damaged by the embezzlement. My friend will find it difficult to trust anyone again since he and his business partner were very good friends for a long time. All because of a character flaw of unrighteousness.

The business partner now experiences the shame of damaging the friendship, the business, the example of Jesus, and most importantly, the guilt associated with the decision made to embezzle. Shame and guilt is all that is left of the friendship.

Love can move people to come to Jesus, but training in righteousness changes character toward making right decisions. Love will not train a person in righteousness. Love is the open door or beginning path toward righteousness if a person chooses.

Shame and guilt penetrates our society. The pain associated with guilt and shame tends to be hidden inside the walls of the human heart.
Disciplining children is a difficult task. Instead of telling our children they are smarter than the mistake they made, we ridicule them with the shame and guilt of making the mistake. We should tell them we are trying to make them successful; and the mistake they just made is not going to make them successful.

Of course, the opposite is true too. Some parents believe not disciplining their children will remove the shame and guilt the parents felt growing up. This is also a destructive pattern. Consequences for unrighteous actions are not experienced. This creates an individual with no sense of his or her actions being capable of causing destruction and pain with either themselves or others.

How is it churches easily call people to love but do not call people to be righteous? How is it churches easily call people to love but not help people find the faith God is trying to instill through their challenges? Love is only the beginning. The Bible says if there is fear, there is no love, but in proverbs, fear is the beginning of knowledge. JOB had no fear of confronting God over the situation so therefore he had love for God.

JOB's character did not become what it was because he first loved. His character was refined with righteousness and faith by obedience to the law. His desire to be utterly righteous even to the point of making sacrifices just in case his children sinned brought about his love for God and people. With Jesus, we need to work backwards. We experience God's love through Jesus' sacrifice for us. We feel love for God and other people. We must move on from milk to solid food - from trying to love more to learning and practicing righteousness and faith. Learning to love more is a product of being more righteous - if we understand the love of Jesus – because it is right to do. What are you willing to do?

Dying Before Denying

JOB 6:8-10
Oh, that I might have my request,
   that God would grant what I hope for,
that God would be willing to crush me,
   to let loose his hand and cut off my life!
Then I would still have this consolation —
   my joy in unrelenting pain —
   that **I had not denied the words of the Holy One**.

I want to start out by referring to the "Book of the Five Rings" by Miyamoto Musashi. A saying in the Japanese Samurai Swordsman culture describes the "Way of the Warrior" is to mean death. This means choosing death whenever there are choices between life and death.

A weaker saying is "To die with your intention unrealized is to die uselessly." The Way of the Warrior is to believe that staying alive after having failed in your intention is the way of the coward. Every man wants to stay alive, but staying alive having failed is a useless absurd point of view. To finish life by living out your intention is what living life is all about. For a Japanese Samurai Warrior that would be death. Then you can pass through life with no possibility of failure. You can perform your life properly."

Another concept ingrained in the Japanese culture of the Samurai is to understand complete selflessness as the cornerstone of being a trusted and complete individual. "If an individual does nothing but think earnestly of his or her lord's welfare, then he or she rises above concern for his or her own welfare and wisdom appears, which is independent of thought. Even knowing this concept, however, it is difficult for most people to rise above thinking of their own welfare.

When you begin something, fix your intention and throw out selfishness and you cannot fail."

Jails are riddled with individuals who have been accused falsely living out their lives paying for something they never committed. Being falsely accused brings out very strong emotions of vindication, justification, and exoneration for the need of acquittal. Even though our lives are riddled with sin, the overriding feeling of being right to prove innocence could eventually overshadow and blind us to the sin that runs rampant in our souls brought about as pride.

Countless stories still exist that portray the idea of people willing to die for something. After Jesus died, people were willing to die before denying Jesus. They were being thrown into cages with lions, cut in two, and a variety of other harsh tortures. The apostles died horrific deaths, except for John, who was described as being sent to an island. If the island were the same island as in the TV series LOST, then I would say it was torture.

Wallace in the movie Braveheart was willing to die for freedom. If my memory serves me, he yelled out the word 'freedom' while his head was being cut off. In the movie The Avengers, Iron Man was willing to die for the cause of saving the planet from the extra-terrestrial invasion.

Why would you risk your life for something that 'may' be real? Why would JOB be willing to die before denying God if there was no evidence of God in his life – just a bunch of laws to obey? There had to be a spiritual contact, connection, or experience for anyone to act in this way. JOB's heart extended beyond obeying the laws and into the realm of relationship.

Even in the Old Testament, people would see a cloud of fire, pass through the ocean on dry land, and see water come from a rock, the earth open up and swallow the faithless who rebelled against God and Moses. Moses had the relationship with God, the people did not.

We deny God almost on a daily basis through a variety of means. This means we make something else more important than God does. Sometimes we fall back on just obeying the laws. We decide to sin. We have attitudes. Our hearts are deceived in a multitude of ways. How could someone who has tasted the goodness of God, the incredible good news of the kingdom in heaven, God revealing himself in his or her life, the changes to their own life, then decide to slide back into disobedience denying the words of God? I have watched this happen to many people.

JOB was willing to die before he denied the Holy One. There are many things in life worth dying for – to save your children, to save your own life (Luke 9), saving another's life, and fighting for freedom. How do so many Christians miss this concept of being willing to die before denying God? I have never even heard it preached from the pulpit in the 20 years I have been a Christian.

To be unwilling to deny God is not really part of church doctrine unless living in a country where Christians are killed for being Christians. Denying God includes more than living in those countries. Denying God includes denying he exists, has control, works in people's life, works in all circumstances, works for the good of people, just to name a few.

Few people believe that denying God comes in to play when viewing pornography, lying, cheating, stealing, etc. because we replace God with those images, thoughts, and patterns.

What if you underwent the same situation JOB went through for no reason? Would you deny God? Or, would you pity yourself because of the belief that your sin caused the events to take place? Of course, just about all of us are not even close to the character of JOB.

Many have gone through instances of devastation not even close to JOB and have denied God. Can we really compare something like divorce as being close to what JOB experienced? Divorce is a decision on our part and not something that has been thrown at us, but people walk away from God because of it.

We can find all kinds of excuses to walk away from God. Are any of them valid? What do you get by walking away from obedience to God? Sure, you get peace from the devastation for a short time, but is it worth not living an eternity in heaven?

Life will always have challenges that come our way. They never stop. It is a constant barrage of situations that cause us to think twice about whether God is good enough. We forget Jesus died on the cross for us just as the Israelites forgot the miracle of the Red Sea opening up for them to cross over safely from the Egyptians. These challenges increase our faith though if we remain true.

Before becoming a Christian, I came across multitudes of people claiming to be Christian and somehow I knew that smoking, cussing, getting drunk, having sex before marriage, and a multitude of other sins did not seem to fit the life of a Christian.

When I became a Christian, I realized I had been right. Now being a Christian, I realize there is a difference between living daily in sin versus committing them out of weakness. Still, the multitude believe they are saved by grace and do not need to work on humbling themselves by repenting before God and asking for forgiveness, receiving healing, and striving for righteousness. Afterward, the repentance should show by making righteous decisions.

Even further, some claiming to be Christian do not believe that living with those sins is a denial of God. JOB was willing to die before denying God and atoned for his sins and the sins of his children. The most intriguing part of all of this is that Jews believe there is no afterlife. JOB was willing to be completely obedient, willing to die before denying God, even though he believed he would not exist after he died. This is utterly astounding.

People need a purpose for living and we all try to find this purpose in an occupations, careers, professions, situations, responsibilities, activities, affairs, or duties. If the purpose of life is to live and die and that is all there is (as the Jews believe), what would be the purpose of following the law, maintaining integrity, honesty, truthfulness, and character traits that are difficult to work on? Wouldn't it be easier to do what you wanted because there are no consequences especially after death?

People have good lives stealing to become wealthy. They have what they want. Sure, a few are caught. You could murder someone to conceal your sin, as we see many times in movies and in real life. A person might be caught and have to go to jail, but many are not caught, and sometimes other people go to jail for a crime they did not commit.

So, if after we die and we go off into oblivion never to exist again, what is the point of living with a law maintaining integrity? Why would a God give us laws to abide by and then not let us exist after being obedient to them? Many people who do not abide by the law live a good life. Where is the advantage to living within the law if we just go into oblivion?

Consequences come from laws that man has put upon himself to try to establish some kind of order and control within society. The concept of having good character traits becomes worthless, without value, and nonsensical when believing a person will not continue to live after death, especially since the corrupt and honorable can live the same good and comfortable life.

We all have an inner desire, planted in our heart by God, as it says in Ecclesiastes, to live an eternity. Why would we have this eternal desire if we were not meant to live an eternity? Is God just playing with our hearts? Is God so cold to put eternity in our hearts and then say, "I was just kidding." The God I know is not that way Old Testament or New Testament.

Let us think about living an eternity for a moment. Would we like to live an eternity with "corrupt" or "honorable people?" Eternity with corruption or unrighteousness is not a placed I would like to be forever. Living, always looking over your shoulder for danger, would not be fun. However, most of us instinctively know we must get along with people and treat them right, which takes some kind of order and control in society.

Still we know we are going to die. Dying and existing no more conflicts with the sense of eternity in our hearts and causes confusion. If we are not Christians walking as God asks, life becomes simple movements to get what we can out of life and live comfortably, since life ends and we are no more. Well, except for the false truth that everyone goes to heaven. Many believe they will go to heaven no matter how they live.

If we are Christians, the very idea of eternity gives us the strength to keep trying to live as God calls us – righteous and loving. When we accept eternity, our strength to be honorable increases. JOB 3:13-14 shows JOB more than likely did not believe in the concept of eternity to give him strength. That would present JOB as honorable even in the midst of believing there was no eternity. A very tall order to fill on anyone's part.

Living as a Christian, I am haunted with the thought of dying for Christ and never denying God. Ten of the original disciples who walked with Jesus died horrifically. I pray every day that I will not have to go through such torment. Believing I have the strength not to deny God is uncertain even knowing eternity is waiting.

JOB's torture is beyond my understanding. I wonder how did he maintain the state of mind and heart to not deny or curse God? JOB's desire to die before he denied God should be a concept driven through Christian culture. However, JOB was not faithful enough to believe or have the strength to hope for a good outcome since he wanted never to have been born.

I propose, as God does, that JOB was a very unique person among men. To understand how he had the strength not to deny God would be beneficial to all true seekers of God. Who of you are willing to live a Christian life?

I am reminded of a story of two guys who come into a church dressed in black with masks and brandishing semi-automatic rifles. One man yells out at the top of his lungs as service was taking place "anyone who calls themselves a Christian and stays in church will die. Those who are not Christians may leave and your life will be spared." Several hundred people left the church leaving only a handful behind. The riflemen closed the doors to the church, took off their masks, laid down their weapons and called out to those that were left "now that we have the true followers of Jesus here, let's worship God"

Protecting our life and family will at times mean denying God on certain levels. Some will choose to sin such as lying or deceiving to make sure their lifestyle stay together as they have planned it. The Old Testament contains a multitude of stories with people lying to protect themselves from destruction. We take God out of the picture when we do that. I am sure we can learn to trust more that God will protect us, which is a scary thought at times.

Through all this torment, JOB has an incredible thought. He is distressed that his last days in life will have no meaning. JOB's mindset is to have meaning throughout his entire life. Dying, as he believes he is, in the state he is in, leaves no room for any kind of meaning. We are privy to the incredible account of JOB now. Obviously, JOB was not aware of the impact he would have with his story, of which is in the Bible.

Finding meaning in life makes life worth living. Living to die is the samurai way. Dying before denying God has meaning to living life eternal. JOB left us with this incredible meaning to life.

As a Christian, we desire to have impact on others. We desire to have impact on this life somehow. We want to live for a reason, a purpose, and a dream, anything that produces meaning. The Bible says the biggest impact anyone can have is to impact a person to make a commitment to follow Christ, become a disciple, and get baptized signifying turning over every aspect of his or her existence to ensure life has meaning and eventually make it to a new life in heaven. But, what kind of meaning would life have if you helped other people to attain eternal life but missed it yourself?

I had several Christian friends who helped many people commit their lives to God through bringing them to church, studying the Bible with them, or allowing someone else to study the Bible with them. Not long afterward, my friends who had helped many people come to God went back to their old ways of living in sin. The proverb rings true; Proverbs 21:18 *"The wicked become a ransom for the righteous, and the unfaithful for the upright."*

I have also heard that if someone truly has the Holy Spirit from baptism, there is no way for him or her to lose it. Many people believe they must not have had the spirit to begin with. Unfortunately, this assumption is wrong. King Saul had the Holy Spirit and ended his life without it. If God is the same and always will be the same, then the Holy Spirit is the same and will always be the same.

Jeremiah is a very sad book to read. He preached a long time affecting no one. It is no wonder he was lamenting the way he was. I would be the same way if I felt I had no impact anywhere. I have to remind myself constantly that whether or not I see where I am having an impact in this life, I am having an affect somewhere. I just cannot always see it. Affecting people moves our heart and brings meaning to life though.

Asking God to help us affect people is a good prayer, but asking God to help us not deny him is a better prayer. The prayer reaches to the core of who we are and who we believe God is. God is always there for us and will never leave us alone. Sometimes, this is a troubling concept for Christians.

God is always there when we sin by choice or by accident. This can be comforting or discomforting because you cannot get away from God. On the comforting side, we feel his presence, which forces us to repent, say sorry, forgive, ask for forgiveness, and lift the burden of guilt. On the discomforting side, JOB was distraught, embittered, and emotionally confused because he obviously had a relationship with God where they communicated with each other. While JOB is going through all this confusion, God is quiet. We become discomforted when God is quiet.

When God is quiet, this is the single most challenging concept in our lives as Christians. We cannot see what lies ahead. We do not understand the reason for the quietness. We feel left alone. We are not sure where to take our next step. In the mist of writing this book, I am looking for a job. God has been quiet. No jobs have presented themselves. I am left with writing and completing this book, of which I really want to do, but as a family, I feel I need to do my part in supporting us. God has always provided in the past, so why am I working so hard to find a job when clearly God has been quiet in this area. This challenges my soul.

Sometimes, quietness from God brings with it the idea that we may be in sin. So, I search my life as does JOB did and asked, "Why have you not pardoned my sin and brought me work?" Sin does not bring God's quietness though. Yes, sin separates us from God, but we step away not hearing.

In JOB's situation, this was not the case. God's belief and faith were still in JOB even while being quiet. This is the same with our life as well. God still believes and has faith in us.

This brings me to think about what it was that compelled JOB to offer the sacrifices for sin just in case someone in his family 'might' have sinned. We have Christ that compels us. What was compelling JOB? Was it God's personal relationship with JOB? How was JOB able to think in such a way? I certainly do not think that way. Did God personally train JOB and is the reason why JOB was so incredible?

I look at my life and realize it took death to get me to stop sinning. Did JOB decide that paying the price for sin was too much? I am talking about the sacrifices of sheep, goats, pigeons, etc for sins committed. During that time in life, a person had to reduce their possessions of sheep, goats, pigeons, grains, and oils when they sinned. If they kept sinning, they would become poor from sacrificing all their animals and food.

I believe this is why JOB was so prosperous. He sinned less. Other individuals also have been prosperous as we see in the story of the rich young ruler whom Jesus talks to. Therefore, it is thought that if someone were to not sin, he or she would become prosperous. The laws of God are at work providing a way to be prosperous.

This concept permeates the culture of the Israelites. Do not sin and be prosperous. JOB had to sin less, to be prosperous. The rich young ruler had to sin less to be prosperous. The Israelites believed you are considered Godly if you were prosperous because the concept that you sin less coincides with the concept of prosperity.

Today, we know we have consequences to our sin. These consequences are vague – what are they? Sometimes they are in your face where you can see them. Some consequences do not come for quite a while. Some show themselves in your character. Since our consequences are vague in many instances, our attention to sin can lack as the scripture points out in Hebrews 12:4 *"In your struggle against sin, you have not yet resisted to the point of shedding your blood."* Consequences become more than just reducing your possessions, *"My son, do not make light of the Lord's discipline, and do not lose heart when he rebukes you, because the Lord disciplines the one he loves, and he chastens everyone he accepts as his son."* Consequences have become thought of as discipline from God.

At times, when I am in sin and have not repented, my wife's attitude changes drastically. The consequences of my sin not only affect me, but others too. I cannot tell if my heart sees more critically because of my sin or if I am affecting people by my change in heart caused by my unrepentant sin. Still, the consequences exist on a vague level possibly causing disharmony within my family occasionally.

Our spirit is affected by the consequences of our sin. We have negative feelings, feel other people are combative, feel other people do not listen to us, feel alone, separated, feel we are the only ones with this type of sin, and all we have to do is ask for forgiveness from Christ on the cross to see and feel change.

Once we take responsibility, admit our sin, and ask for forgiveness, the pain subsides, the burden gets relieved, the heart calms down, and we find new life as we come out of the darkness and back into a lightened spirit. We regain our spirit of joy, peace, friendship, and love not only with God, but also with other people.

In Old Testament times, the consequences to sin cost the individual something of physical value. They had to sacrifice an animal or something. The consequences of sin were to lose valuable property of your family unit. Therefore, if you did not want to reduce your property, you would choose to sin less. I think this is where the belief comes from that if you were prosperous then you sinned little. You did not spend your resources on your sins. For those not so prosperous, you obviously must be in sin.

If people would not consider their sins, then God would ultimately force them into being conquered by the nations around them.

Willing to die before denying God is a tough calling. We must constantly work on our character by sinning less and producing righteousness. We should be praying for God to forgive our family's sin 'just in case they sinned' so we can get a sense of JOB's heart for others. This is easy to say and write, but not so easy to put into practice as I have found in my own life. However, I want to be considered by God as God considered JOB "there is no on like him." So, I keep striving to do what I can to change. Hopefully, I will get to the point JOB was. I can do without the massive testing though. God already has shown what I mean to him through Christ. It is now up to me to change.

Our lives should be examples of recognizing sin, coming clean at every failure, and do our best to remove sin from our lives. Living like JOB is what Jesus meant when he said in Matthew 5:20, *"For I tell you that unless your righteousness surpasses that of the Pharisees and the teachers of the law, you will certainly not enter the kingdom of heaven."* Pharisees paid strict attention to the law. Yes, they made their own traditions to go along with it, but were vigilant in following the laws. Unfortunately, love was missing. Some people believe you can smoke and drink excessively and still be called a Christian. Pharisees had the heart to follow every law to the letter – to exceed this is to apply love.

Jesus came to fulfill the law not abolish it. Bringing them together is what Jesus came to do; and bringing them together in harmony was the goal. Could love exist without righteousness? Righteousness stems from the laws and compassion stems from love. God did not stop believing in the law he so adamantly defended in the Old Testament. JOB had both the law and love. We have the same chance to have both as well.

We cannot take our Christian walk for granted. We must have the heart to recognize sin, confess our committed sins to God and each other, repent when we do sin by begging God for forgiveness, forgive ourselves, and strive to avoid sin and not deny God. So, who among you want to live like the Samurai for Jesus?

Wet Sandwich

Who likes being wrong? I do not know anyone that likes being wrong. Being wrong is humbling. We all like to be in the right because it makes us feel good about ourselves.

Our school system is designed to ensure we believe we have the right answer. The system does not come from a standpoint of formulating questions around a problem to find an answer. We are driven to be right from a young age. We must get the answers right on a test to get the best score of 100. When we play sports, we learn to make the right decision about our actions. Being right all the time is an alarming thing though.

Taking the stance of being the knowledgeable person and knowing the right answer rather than learning to ask questions before expressing our knowledge, is detrimental to knowing the full picture, and is not the personality of a humble person. We all fall for the lie of always being right. JOB's friends fell into this trap and refused to listen to JOB.

But, who wants to listen to people? We love talking about ourselves. Few people have figured out that listening is a powerful tool. I have had a difficult time learning to listen. I am quick to answer most of the time.

Of course, having children causes a person to have the right answer all the time too. I work on asking my children questions and listening to them. I want them to feel heard. I want them to come to me for the answers to their questions, but I question them about their questions. In my answers to them, I have been wrong at times and had to apologize.

Admitting I was wrong has caused my children to understand I may not be right when I say I am correct. They are only 10 and 11, at this point, and learning quickly. Still, I want them to question the validity of answers, including mine, in every aspect of their life.

JOB's friends came to JOB already knowing what had happened. They formulated assumptions about his situation based upon the laws and character of God. They refused to ask him if he had committed any sin that may have caused the destruction. They immediately went for the throat, saying he was obviously in sin, he refused to recognize his sin, he was prideful thinking he was sinless, and was blinded. Because they assumed they knew the answer to his destruction, their listening ears, minds, and hearts were closed. Sure, it did not help that Satan planted the seed to begin with.

Assumptions, most of the time means being wrong. Assumptions are usually in opposition to listening. When we find ourselves assuming, you can bet that listening was more than likely non-existent. I cannot count how many times I have assumed and have been wrong.

While writing this chapter and other chapters, as I said before, God exposed information for me to consider bringing to light what needs to be said.

I like watching TEDTalks at TED.com. You can find them on Netflix as well. They promote "Ideas Worth Spreading." They are seminars given around the world on specific topics worth exposing. I came across one while writing this chapter from Kathryn Schultz' speech about "On Being Wrong." She researched what people think and believe about being wrong and came up with three levels of assumptions I found to be very eye opening and brilliant.

Kathryn Schultz says, "When you think and feel right, you believe what you feel perfectly reflects reality. When you feel this way, you make assumptions when communicating to others through a series of unfortunate assumptions:

1. **The Ignorance Assumption**
   When we share the truth, the other person will finally step out of ignorance. If it does not work because

those people have the same info we do, then we move to number two.

2. **The Idiocy Assumption**
They have all the same pieces of the puzzle and are too moronic to put them together correctly. When that does not work, we move to three.

3. **The Evil Assumption**
They know the truth and distort the truth for their own malevolent purposes."

Kathryn also stated one of the most brilliant statements I have ever heard. "The miracle of your mind is not that you can see the world as it is. It is so you can see the world as it is not." For those that believe in God, this is the reason why we do what we do – to see the world as it is not – to see the invisible qualities of God – to understand faith – to believe in heaven – to live eternally.

Kathryn goes on to say that always being right will cause us to miss the truth. Our mistakes we make will never be considered as wrong needing correction. This one single act of being right has the potential for people to treat other people horribly. When we believe we are right, we have this idea things are going to happen a certain way, but sometimes something else happens instead. An example is when America went to war in Iraq to find weapons of mass destruction and instead, something else happened.

Being over confident about an assumption opens the door to false wisdom. There is nothing more truer and visually seeable today that exists in every organization in the world.

I have never met a church that believes they are NOT the true way to knowing and having a relationship with God. This confident assumption created by the confidence in the knowledge of reading the Bible confirms the assumption to be true. This vicious circle exists in every denomination. "We know the right way to know and worship God." The reason this exists is the changes, miracles, life transformations, experienced by people are the proof necessary to believe the church is on the right track. But, this happens in all groups. This lays the foundation for the confidence in the assumption creating the circle of uniqueness and ultimately separation from every group until it leads to death that is unless the confidence is changed. However, we all like to be confident in what we know and feel is true.

One of the most destructive positions of being right is through religion. The Catholics believe they are right because they were the first church. The Lutherans believe they are right because they challenged the Catholic position of only the priests being able to read the Bible. The Presbyterians, the Baptist, the Mormons, the Non-De-Nominationlists, Islam, Hindu, Atheists, and all the others not mentioned, believe they are right. However, being "righteous" is almost always never preached or practiced. I would think that if you believe you are right that being righteous is an extension of being right. We also know that love does not equal righteousness. Who is practicing love along with righteousness?

What if we took a position in that people fought about who was the most righteous and loving, faithful, and truthful? Would this change things? Not at all. Jesus calls us to be disciples. We must admit we can be wrong, be a learner, be a listener, not be right but be righteous, and seek truth – not to be right but to be pure, righteous, and holy. Being right is different from being righteous. Being righteous deals with one's character. Being right is projected as proof or validation toward another person.

Many people who claim to be Christian want to be just that – someone who knows about Christ – but are far removed from being disciplined in righteousness. Being Christian in America brings with it a meaning similar to being from a country – I am Brazilian, Spanish, Italian, French, Russian – I am Christian.

Christianity has become like a wet sandwich lying in a puddle of water. The bread is all soggy. It looks like a sandwich. Who wants to eat a wet sandwich? A wet sandwich belief exists in many religious circles, "I have sin living inside of me, so why should I try hard to stop it? God forgives me of my sin anyway. Isn't it all about love anyway?" This type of belief is the wet sandwich Christianity I am talking about.

The day I wrote this chapter I ran into a woman at the school my children go to, which turned out to be a classic example of someone who does not consider righteousness in her walk with Jesus. We started talking and she said she was a nanny for a child because she could earn extra cash money under the table. Her actual income could then be shown as lower, which drops her into a lower income bracket. This allows her to make more money but pay less for her monthly alimony payments. Right after she said this, she mentioned she met the parents of the child at the church she goes to and has the love of Jesus in her. Obviously, she believes it is okay to lie and cheat to earn more money and pay less alimony. She is not alone in this thinking. This is wet sandwich religion. Where is the sense of shame over her sin?

God puts certain scriptures in the Bible that we stay away from because the scripture challenges our very beliefs. One comes to mind that challenges my belief about sin. *"In your struggle against sin, you have not yet resisted to the point of shedding your blood."* (Hebrews 12:4) OUCH! You mean I have to resist sin to the point of shedding my blood? This is the ultimate call to righteousness. Isn't this what JOB did. He was bleeding from all his losses and the painful sores on his physical self and he did not sin. Incredible!

Have you been down on your knees crying and begging God to remove certain sin from your life? Has your desire to be righteous and repent from sin even been close to asking God, "I will do whatever it takes. God, you do what you need to do with me so I can repent from this sin." I do not know many people that would pray such a radical prayer that might entail blood of some sort.

I have prayed radical prayers a few times in my life. I really desired to understand something. A few years into my walk with God, I felt my understanding of Jesus on a cross was shallow. I prayed a radical prayer. I got on my knees and told God, "I feel I am missing something from my understanding of Jesus being on the cross. Please do whatever it takes to help me to understand the meaning of the cross on a deeper level."

Now, you have to understand this leaves the door wide open for God to do whatever it takes. My thinking included things such as being in a car accident and losing limbs or being completely paralyzed from breaking my neck. My mind went all the way to being tortured in some way. I ran around for a month being very fearful and aware of everything around me. I knew my prayer would be answered, but did not know how or when. My heart so desired to know Jesus on a deep level no matter what the consequences were though.

Then it came. Fortunately, God brought about a dream that brought me closer to what Jesus did for me. I do not believe it was the complete and final understanding of knowing Jesus, but it did bring me closer to an understanding of Jesus on the cross.

In my dream, my father and my uncle, people who I looked up to, without reason, were standing over Jesus with bats about to beat Jesus. Jesus was kneeling with his eyes to the ground waiting for the beating. I screamed with every ounce of strength I had at my uncle and dad to stop the madness. They just smiled back at me.

Jesus turned his eyes up, looked at me, and told me without words, "I am doing this for you." I awoke in a sweat and violently wreathing in my bed. It broke my heart my uncle and dad would do that, but then it moved my heart - I did that to Jesus as well. My understanding did not come from knowledge of right or wrong but from a heart of caring to understand who and what Jesus did to the point of praying a radical prayer.

I have challenged people to pray radical prayers, and just about everyone refuses because of some sort of fear. Jesus prayed a radical prayer in the Garden of Gethsemane, *"Not as I will, but as you will."* Isn't this the basic lifestyle of a Christian though – not me, but you God?

Few of us live out this lifestyle on a daily basis. If we did, our desire would be to ask God to remove sin and help us to become righteous, to know the truth, be accountable, have faith, and to love deeply. Isn't fighting sin to the point of shedding blood a radical idea? We have the mistaken belief that God forgives sin so why would anyone fight sin to the point of blood. JOB not only fought sin in his own life, but the lives of his children. JOB claimed he did not allow himself to even lust after a woman – inconceivable, but a type of heart worth imitating.

Our beliefs take shape when we are young and continue to be shaped throughout our lifetime. Beliefs are reinforced by circumstances in our life. We learn right from wrong fairly easily if someone is willing to take the time to teach us. If someone is not willing to take the time to be with us and teach us, we can come to an unconscious understanding we are not loved.

False beliefs are created while we are young and are in opposition to what God offers when we become Christian.

We believe we are unloved, but God says we are loved. Those two belief systems exist within us conflict with each other. Changing behavior is nearly impossible when two belief systems exist. The easy one will win all the time unless we fight back. It is easier to believe we are not loved and to live as such.

False beliefs need to be identified and dealt with. I was lucky to have my false beliefs identified so I could work on changing my behavior. When I was young, I had the mistaken belief that when I was confronted with intense situations, I could go to a safe place I had created. I believed that was the right thing to do. The false belief was pointed out to me. I found out other false beliefs were attached. I had been sabotaging myself believing love did not hurt. I created a belief I was pathetic and unlovable because people hurt me. I felt I was right about the belief because of the circumstances in my life that pointed to and encouraged the belief.

Because I believed I was unlovable, I would not let people in my life to love me. I created a wall between myself and other people to keep them away.

As I said before, beliefs are the core strength of any person. When we have weak beliefs, we can be tossed by the wind by every changing situation. (Ephesians 4:14) Some have beliefs so strong they will strap explosives around themselves and blow themselves up for a cause. Others believe they can get away with lying to the public about the status of a company (Enron) and get away with it. Our beliefs change daily through the circumstances going on around us. This is the reason why Satan targets our beliefs either through pure evil or by masquerading as an angel of light. Even Satan's servants masquerade as angels of light. (2 Corinthians 11:14-15)

My false beliefs prevented me from making righteous decisions, truly learn what love is, understand how to increase my faith, accept accountability, and grasp the truth. My pride gets in the way believing I am right in my false beliefs. That is until they are broken.

Thousands of people, including myself, have benefited from a program called Grief Recovery.com. The course is exactly what the name describes – recovery from grief in life. We all have some sort of grief we are dealing with and as young children, we automatically grieve. As we get older, we learn to not grieve. The program reverses our inability to grieve.

I removed some of my core false beliefs with the program. The reason why I even went was because my wife took the course and changed so dramatically that I HAD to find out what it was all about. I watched many people's lives change because of the power of Grief Recovery. The process targets false belief systems and demolishes them.

Beliefs affect our perception of ourselves, others, and life in general. For instance, my dad was an alcoholic and was in bars drinking most of the time during the important years of my life. I know it had to be tough to raise four kids, but his love for drinking took precedence over spending time with us kids. As he got older, he did spend more time with my younger brother and sister, but I was already out of the house. My perception was created from my belief he loved alcohol more than he love me. Somehow, this caused me to believe I was to blame for being unlovable. I believed I was right about my understanding. On top of that, who needed God when I was unlovable anyway?

My behavior stemmed from my beliefs. My decisions were based upon my beliefs creating the behavior in my life. My actions were dictated by my perceptions. I tried to change my behavior repeatedly without looking at my beliefs. However, trying to change your behavior does not get at the root of the problem. Your behavior has a root cause resting in your beliefs learned through the circumstances in life. The only way to change your behavior is to change your beliefs.

Grief Recovery is one of the most powerful courses to change beliefs. Of course, only the Bible can start you on the right path in the first place of being open to knowing who you are.

Forgiveness is at the forefront of the Grief Recovery. The funny thing is, while Jesus was on the cross, he could have said a multitude of words but chose forgiveness. He could have said, "I love you, or believe in me," or something else, but did not. By using the term "forgiveness," we need to focus on this aspect in order to change our beliefs.

Opening the door to our soul and to heaven does not mean everyone will instantly be healed. This would negate the idea of what type of individual we need to be before God – "disciple." You see, the word "Christian" does not imply being "disciplined." Being a disciple brings with it the idea of being disciplined. It is easier to live as a Christian because you do not need to be disciplined in righteousness, faith, obedience, accountability, truth, and love. Christians can just live without the burden of being disciplined because it is all about Christ's love for us.

This type of thinking is the false belief "all we need to do is accept Christ's love" for us. Christ died for me therefore; all I have to do is let him love me. Love takes two, not one. Love is an action. Christ gave all he had for us. If we are to imitate Christ, we are to give all we have for him. Christ was righteous. We need to be righteous. We must respond to his love and allow him to change our false beliefs. This means being a disciple and having a learner's heart open to hearing God's plan for removing the false beliefs in your life not just changing your behavior of appearing to be a good person. A large part of being disciplined is by having someone in your life to help you with your discipline. God speaks through people too. JOB has this heart of a being open to be taught, *"Teach me, and I will be quiet; show me where I have been wrong."*

If we continue in our state of being inactive in love, we learn to believe God remains distant and absent in our lives. If two people like each other, they take the necessary actions to do the things the other person likes and removes the things they do not like. My wife asked me to stop doing quite a few things when we got married. I asked my wife to stop doing things as well. My wife also takes actions toward me with her love for me. I do the same. What if neither of us put forth action in our relationship? What if we did not remove but allowed sin to run rampant in our relationship? What if I said my wife loves me so why should I fight sin? Would we have a relationship? The answer is simple - no. So, why do we believe differently about God with this false belief "he loves us anyway, so why should I refrain from sin?"

Let us come back to the unlovable portion. Why would God want to be there for someone who believes he or she is unlovable? I go through these feelings occasionally believing I am unlovable, especially when I make a decision to sin. My belief changes back to a feeling of being unlovable when I sin.

How could God love someone so sinful – one who decides to sin? God loved me before I even tried to be a disciple; therefore, he still loves now that I am trying to be a disciple. In addition, what I realized is that if I did not "decide" to sin, I felt lovable. Just to be clear, accepting the feeling of being loved came after I broke my false beliefs and perceptions through forgiveness.

One thing we can take comfort in is being wrong about our beliefs. Accepting the fact we can be wrong is the first step toward recovery in every facet of our lives. Being right is not all it is cracked up to be because believing we are right can be revealed as being wrong.

JOB's friends believed they were right, but were wrong. Our beliefs about ourselves can be wrong but can be made right through forgiveness and resisting sin. JOB was not "right" but "righteous." Jesus opens the door for us to understand God loves us, break our false beliefs, become righteous, find truth, become obedient, seek accountability, increase faith, and exercise love in our lives.

Luke 7:47 says, "*Whoever has been forgiven little loves little.*" If we only seek forgiveness for a few of our sins, our understanding of love remains shallow. If we seek forgiveness to the core of our beliefs, change our perceptions, and then our behaviors, we realize the destructive power of those beliefs and our gratitude for God increases along with our depth of understanding about love and righteousness. Love opens the doorway to be righteous and faithful. JOB had the qualities that God boasted about. So, let us make a new sandwich and throw out the wet sandwich and make a meal that is worthy of God's praise.

Freedom of Choice

Opposing forces gives life movement and balance. Our ability to choose stems from opposing forces. In the beginning, there was light and dark, good and evil - giving us the ability to choose. If there were only good, where would the choice be? Everything is good. There is no need for choice. No need to consider the outcome of a decision. Everything is taken care of and is considered good. However, we would not describe it as good because "what is" would just be "what is" – without label. God allowed good and evil to exist, and we became like God by eating the forbidden fruit. (Genesis 1) We need to have these opposites in our life so our conscience can reason.

We lived in a perfect world before the fall of Adam and Eve and could not accept it. All they had to do is be obedient. All you have to do is be obedient too. Are you doing that? What are your choices? God allowed an imperfect world because in a perfect world, we would not need to do whatever it takes to get out of the dark world. In a perfect world, there would be no freedom of choice. In an imperfect world, we must choose righteousness and love over death from our sin.

Laws tell us certain actions are not acceptable in society or by God, and everyone should abide by them. If we went around and obeyed every law exactly as it is written, we would spend most of the time looking up laws to determine if we are following them.

Through the Israelites, God brought his law. Through Jesus, forgiveness and love came to fulfill the law and, of course, release us from the law. Therein lies much of the confusion.

The light came to the dark for balance. Evil came in opposition to good for balance. Joy balances despair. We have both opposing sides bringing shape to our lives and to bring freedom of choice. It is one of the many gifts from God.

On a side note, two types of 'sorry' exist. The first apology is to say sorry to someone for hurting him or her. The other type of apology is to say sorry to someone even though we did not hurt him or her. The person is experiencing some type of pain. By saying sorry to them, we are giving them compassion. We will not feel their pain, but we can say we feel for them. Most people know this, but I did not.

When I became a married man, I had to learn the second apology. I was excited because I could tell people I cared for them through this word. My usual actions up to that point were to serve them in their time of distress and pain. My ability to replace brake shoes on cars was one of the ways I served to try to tell people I cared for them. When someone was in pain from inner turmoil, I was at a loss of what to do until I learned about the second apology.

I look back at my conversion to Christianity and wonder if I told God I am sorry for my sin before I was baptized. I know I received forgiveness for sin. I wanted to be considered worthy of God and for him to change my life radically. Jesus atoned for my sin even though I probably did not say sorry to him for my sin.

Atoning for sin, as in the Jewish culture, is a way of bringing a sense of awareness to sin. Years of sinning and atoning for sin can make someone become fully aware of sin and feel sorry when it happens repeatedly. Sometimes atoning just becomes mechanical though. For gentiles, we do not have atonement ingrained in our lives.

As a young Christian, when I sinned, I would pray for God to help me fight to stay away from sin. The fear of God moved me to try harder because I did not want to endure the consequences of my sin. The environment I was in at church promoted this type of disciplining of character.

First, I just accepted God's forgiveness of my sin. Years later, I somehow started praying for God to forgive my sin. Even later, I moved to a point of saying sorry for my sin while asking for forgiveness. I had a progression from fighting sin to saying sorry to God for my sin because I kept sinning. I suppose my Christian friends had told me to say sorry to God, but the concept certainly did not sink in until later in life. On top of that, the concept saying sorry to God was not preached from the pulpit, only asking forgiveness.

Once I learned to take full responsibility for my actions of sinning, it became easier to say sorry for my sin to God and others. I then started being able to remove sin from my life. Forgiving myself then became a new process of repenting.

What is our life if we refuse to take responsibility for our sin, apologize, and repent? Many of us can look back and see what our life would be like if we had not made the decision to let Jesus affect our hearts and life. Everyone I know makes wrong decisions whether or not you follow Jesus. Atoning for your sin is a daily decision not a yearly one.

At times, I do not want to, but I do, make decisions that tear my life down, my heart down, my family down, and my friends down. At times, the sin that lives inside of me takes over, and I do not have control over it. The most difficult thing to do is to forgive myself. I have to work at forgiveness. I know God forgives me when I admit and apologize for my sin, but forgiving myself is a different story because I believe I can do better than that. I put undo pressure on myself.

I sometimes tear myself down when I sin believing I am trying to administer justice to myself for my wrongdoing. Somehow, I believe that by doing this, God does not have to administer justice, but that is not the case. God disciplines whom he loves. I get it from both sides, God and myself. I realize I do not need to hammer myself for my sin, but I desire to be righteous. Paul talked about beating his body into submission. I feel I am trying to make my body submit. I have done well in many areas. I have a lot of work to go. Because I have been given the freedom from God to make righteous or unrighteous decisions, my character is getting stronger in making the right choice.

Very few churches I have been to challenge its members to be righteous, make righteous decisions, and live a righteous life. Many churches preach love. Sermons center on love. Love will change everything in life if you just love better, more, sacrificially, and from the heart. People come and want to hear love, but if challenged to be righteous, they get upset, angry, and even leave.

Many believe that if you just love more, righteousness will flourish in your heart. Love is awesome, but what happens is people do not learn to make decisions to obey God's laws while making decisions to love. Jesus never abolished the laws, and we need laws. Somehow, laws have become polar opposite to love because they are legalistic in nature.

During my first four years as a single Christian, I had a chance to date women with the knowledge of God's laws and the love of Jesus inside me. God's laws dictated I treat the women I dated with respect, without being physical or sexual at all, and learn to encourage them. I dated as much as I could because I wanted to learn what God wanted me to learn about relationships.

Through my friends, who were learning as I was, I learned creative ways of encouraging a sister in the lord. One time I went to the extent of asking a sister out a month ahead of time. I went around, asked all her friends what they thought of the sister, and asked them to say something encouraging. I typed down what was said about her and gave it to her on the date. I had never seen joyful crying before. I was open to dating righteously and with advice.

What I learned from this experience was dating with pure motives. Sisters were not hurt by my actions. I learned to listen to their hearts and understand what encouraged them. The trust between the sisters and me I dated kept growing because I told them I respect and honor them.

When I met my wife, during our initial dating, which was in accordance with God's laws and done in purity, she would leave messages on my answering machine that were so encouraging, I saved them, well, until they filled up my machine. I then spent time and effort typing them down filling 17 pages of paper and gave them to her when I asked her to be my girlfriend.

We went to a restaurant with our friends who had helped me and gave me advice on every move I made in dating her. The messages were so encouraging I read a few of them before I asked her to be my girlfriend. The reason they were so encouraging was that she had learned to listen to my heart through our non-physical contact during dating as I listened to her heart. The anticipation of the first kiss was when she was in her wedding gown, with a ring on her finger, that I put there. It was intense and full of ecstasy. It was my freedom of choice to act this way. Only a small percentage of people actually experience pure relationships before marriage, which is a gift from God.

My wife and I were excited to have this treasure from God by being connected in mind, heart, and soul before being connected physically after being married. It set a solid foundation for our marriage. It was our choice to be righteous and pure and God blessed it.

Whenever I talk to Christians I encounter, I find out purity and righteousness is not the norm when dating. Many people who call themselves Christians have physical relations with each other and do not adhere to God's laws of purity. They have been taught that being physical or sexual is a decision between two people and not from God. They have been taught that if you love someone, love covers over the sin of sexual immorality. Righteousness is not even part of the lifestyle of those Christians.

I encountered Christians who believe they can sin and not be held accountable to God or their church family because it is all about love, not righteousness. Righteousness and faith is the key to making it to heaven – love is only part of the equation. God gave us freewill to choose our path.

Where does Romans 6:2 come into the lives of a Christian? *"By no means! We are those who have died to sin; how can we live in it any longer?"* In order to understand what sin is, we must understand the law. Galatians 5:19-21 says, *"The acts of the flesh are obvious: sexual immorality, impurity and debauchery; idolatry and witchcraft; hatred, discord, jealousy, fits of rage, selfish ambition, dissensions, factions and envy; drunkenness, orgies, and the like. I warn you, as I did before, that those who live like this will NOT inherit the kingdom of God."* This is a call to righteousness sparked by the love of Jesus. Why do so many miss this scripture? The scripture says you will not inherit the kingdom of God unless you practice righteousness in your life even if you have love.

Sexually immoral laws are contained in Deuteronomy. Understanding the laws in Deuteronomy defines what is being talked about in Galatians. An example is that a person is not to have sexual relations with a sister unless married. If every female is or can be a sister in Christ, then all are sisters until married. Then they take on a different status. If you have sex with your sister before marriage, you will be having sex with someone else's wife. If this were talked about in church, pastors would lose many people in their congregation. Their livelihood would also be at risk because of the drop in income. Following God has a cost that most are not willing to pay.

Accountability is another factor that reduces righteousness to nothingness. JOB held himself accountable for his actions and the actions of his children. Accountability in church is nonexistent mainly because discipling between Christians is nonexistent. This is mainly because the belief exists that accountability is legalistic. How are people going to have their pride and selfishness, things in our character which cannot be seen ourselves, pointed out by others so we can work on removing them from our life, especially since God hates pride? We need others to point it out. Accountability and discipling does that for us. It is our decision to be accountable.

Obedience in church is thrown out the door because love is supposed to cover all sins. Well, except for being obedient to coming to church and giving money. We are free to sin. We are led to believe we do not need to worry so much about obedience. Love does cover over sins, but we cannot use love or freedom as an excuse to sin. (Galatians 5:13) Many pastors do not call people to be obedient. People do not want to be told what to do from other people especially since we have freedom in Christ.

I was told what to do when I first became a Christian and glad I was. However, I felt I was smart enough to understand what I was reading in the Bible, and I did not need others to impose themselves on me. I later found out I was prideful and arrogant. I never considered myself in this manner. I had some really good friends that spoke the truth to me and finally got through to me about my pride. Four of my friends sat around and battered me out of love – wanting me to repent – giving me words of life. I would like to say it was easy. I appreciate my friends for taking the time to give all of their hearts. It was my choice to let them disciple me.

Truth, is another aspect of life reduced to earthworm status because love reigns supreme. Truth needs to be spoken so people can change and grow. Truth does not always feel good though. We are told to speak the truth in love. This has been reduced to a position of telling someone the truth only if it feels good and does not harm or give the other person pain. That is how you love someone. God will teach them therefore, we do not need to express the harsh truths such as, "You have pride and here is why." Obviously, the culture in JOB's day understood it is right to point out pride; just do not try to show people their pride when they are in pain. Talking about pride is difficult to do since the words can come off as unloving and harsh, but is necessary for our godliness. Besides, spiritual "blows and wounds" come from true friends.

Speaking the truth when we know it will not feel good to the other person shows our complete love for them. We show we care if they are being righteous. We show we care about their godliness. Unfortunately, we are told not to hurt the other person even if it is the truth. We do not love when we do this. We should never try to speak the truth if it is going to hurt someone else because it is NOT a loving gesture. This is how we end up with a wet sandwich Christian fellowship as stated in the previous chapter.

The act of serving has become the act of worshipping God. We are told we must serve and sacrifice more so we can love more and be more like Jesus. Granted, that is true. However, this becomes the staple diet of Christians. Churches place serving and sacrifice as being more important than righteousness. We see in the following scripture that righteousness is the first word of our pursuit. *"But you, man of God, flee from all this, and pursue **righteousness**, godliness, faith, love, endurance and gentleness."* (1 Timothy 6:11) *"Flee the evil desires of youth and pursue*

righteousness, *faith, love and peace, along with those who call on the Lord*" (2 Timothy 2:22)

Righteousness takes work though. Righteousness takes atonement, truth, obedience, accountability, sacrifice, faith, and love all practiced at the same time. They are inseparable. They work together in unison and in harmony. One cannot live without the other.

Satan's great lie is to get us only to believe we need love and nothing else. Everything will fall into place if we learn to love better. Is a half-truth the whole truth?

Some say, "who can be righteous?" JOB was righteous as well as Abel, Noah, Zacharias and Elisabeth, and Abraham, to name a few. JOB was righteous to the point of God using him as an example for us to follow. God trusted JOB so much he allowed him to be tested on every level. God did not say JOB had a great love. Would someone who loved greatly want to die and be sent back to the dust of the earth or scorned the day of his birth? God said there was no one like him in righteousness and integrity. God was proud of JOB. God was amazed at JOB. God was confident in JOB.

The death of Jesus came to offer us a doorway into righteousness. To love greatly but still live as those who live in Galatians 5:19 is in direct conflict to righteousness. To remove sin takes making the right decisions even to the point of blood. If the death of someone is not enough to move someone toward righteousness, then the heart has been hardened by sin's deceitfulness. We are given the choice.

When family members die, we are moved to express our feelings – whatever they may be. When my father died, my heart was not compassionate. My father had emphysema from smoking 50 years of his life. He lost most of his lung capacity to breathe normal. Near the end of his life, he was only able to walk about 20 feet before he would start panting heavily.

My dad decided one day to stop eating and was prepared to die. I remember coming to see him in his bed and not knowing what to say. Even on his deathbed. I was very uncompassionate because of the relationship we did not have. I knew very little about him as a person. I knew he gave his best and he loved me, but he had a fascination with alcohol that overtook him in his efforts to relate to me. My father had not decided to be righteous in his life. Our relationship was one-sided. I always called him to see what was going on, but he never called me. My dad was suffering intensely. I offered no compassion just as JOB's friends did not.

In my effort to be righteous, my love had lost some of its value toward others. I could love those who loved me, but I had a difficult time loving those who I did not know and were suffering, such as my dad. I am grateful for my dad for the things he did do for me. I just did not know him like I wanted to. He never opened up about his childhood.

I learned from my grandmother that he was a child shunned by his father. I do not blame him for finding alcohol as a way out of the pain. I also took that same route for a while for the pain I felt in lacking the relationship with my dad. I thank God for finding me and putting me through the fires of change.

God is multifaceted and not only love. Love is the glue that sticks everything together creating a perfect way of life. Practicing love without the others facets is a waste of time and not what God intended. The same happens with coming into a relationship with God.

Some believe all you have to do is believe and be "immersed" into Christ. The Bible talks about both types of "immersion" – of the heart and of the water. The Bible also says to make a disciple first and then baptize them. Why is it believed you can baptize without this "making" first? Making a cake requires several things – flour, eggs, milk, sugar, etc. Making a disciple takes time, effort, love, challenging, praying, and making the right choices, and finally commitment into a lifestyle you have learned about and the expectations involved. A person cannot commit to a lifestyle if they do not know what the expectations are. However, belief is the first step. Baptism is the final step after being prepared to do so.

Our society is based on a diet mentality. Just eat this and you will lose weight. There is no lifestyle change. The weight comes back or physical problems develop in lieu of lifestyle change. Our society also has what I call a fast food mentality – I want it now as quick as I can get it.

Learning a new lifestyle of a Christian is NOT microwavable in eight seconds. Walking and talking as a Christian takes a thorough knowledge of the commitment involved and a heart change. Sure, a person can commit to learning what is expected, but the final commitment is baptism – complete immersion both physical and mental, complete obedience, and complete commitment.

The Bible does not say baptize a person and then teach them how to be a disciple. This is the easy way and does not take much work on our part as a Christian. Why would anyone want to work hard for God? Jesus says the fields are plentiful, but the workers are few. We have freedom of choice to do what we want to do either in obedience or not.

Teaching someone to believe the words in the Bible, to confess sin, to repent of sin, commit to a lifestyle of righteousness, faith, and love requires work on the part of another Christian. Once a person understands what the cross means in their life, that is when love is established and then righteousness and faith must become a part of their life. Love is the doorway. Righteousness and faith is the pathway. Heaven is the goal. To get out of the world of sin is hard work.

We have the freedom to choose everything in our life. We can choose to follow God or not. We can choose love over righteousness or anything else. We can choose to obey the words the way they are stated in the Bible, or not. In the end, our choices dictate whether we find life when we die. No one else has that power over us. If we allow God to help us choose right, we are closer to being righteous.

The Love Syndrome

When the conviction to be righteous dies or ceases to exist in your soul, reliance on the deception that love can save you follows.

In this chapter, I want to focus on a specific type of love. I understand that righteousness combined with love need to be practiced together in order to be holy. My aim is to talk about love for a moment because there are a few different types of love. So, for a moment, I have taken righteousness out of the picture to understand some key points.

In some churches, the main message preached is to love God more and get closer in your relationship with him. What is described though is this feeling we need to have toward God and others. However, it is not the feeling we need to focus on in our walk with God. The reason is that Jesus would never have made it through the cross if he ONLY had a feeling of love for people. Satan has duped us in to believing this feeling is the ultimate in worshipping God.

I cannot count how many times I have heard the same expressions from people, "I do not feel the love of God today." "I just need to get closer to God." "I feel far away from God." "I just need to pray more to feel God's love." These types of statements come from the belief that our feeling about our closeness to God is what counts as worship of him. This idea is that when the 'feeling' is gone, something needs to be done to get that feeling back again.

People throw up their arms in the air trying to receive the feeling. People believe that speaking in unintelligible words or tongues is accessing this feeling of being connected to God. The words of tongues is considered as the language of love or the language of God; is a form of worshiping God;

is a message to let others know you are with God. These feelings have been associated as the way to be connected to and to worship God. However, the emotional feelings alone are not your worship of God nor do they count more than other spiritual things in your life.

I love the game of soccer and still play to this day. I follow European teams, purchase their jerseys, and watch games, watch leagues such as the Championship League, English Premier League, Italian Serie A, and the Spanish league. I love the feeling I get when I play and watch soccer. If the feeling were all I focused on, I would not be playing soccer today. It takes so much more than that to be considered as a player. Love only opens the door.

In order to play soccer, I need to have commitment to playing by the rules, be righteous in my approach toward other players by not purposely harming them in an effort to win the game. I need to look after my own physical health by taking vitamins and supplements, ensuring enough exercise between games to keep endurance and stamina up, practicing moves, stretching, weight training, and a whole slew of other activities just to play the game I love. If I relied only on the feeling I get when I play, I certainly would not be playing at the age I am at now.

I love my wife and my kids. If I did not practice making the right decisions, my family would be a mess, even though I love them. I love being with them, teasing them, wrestling with my kids, watching movies with them, playing soccer, and learning the Bible. I have to do other things with them too. If I just sat at home in a chair and said, "I love you. Go and be well," but never went to the store to buy them clothes or shoes, what does my love say about me to them. Absolutely nothing! I am a clanging cymbal just making noise.

JOB did not only have this feeling of love or connection to God. JOB was recognized for his reverence and his heart to follow and submit to God and his laws. He was a righteous man like no other. JOB did not raise his arms trying to feel the love of God even in his troubles. JOB did not express he must get closer to God, pray harder, or even speak in unintelligible love language. JOB KNEW GOD and GOD KNEW JOB. God knew JOB because of what he practiced in his life not for how much JOB had this feeling of love for God. JOB's desire to be obedient and righteous beyond anyone else is what counted, but stemmed from his love.

Three kinds of love exist in the Bible – (philia) friendship love, (eros) romantic love, and (agape) which is commitment love. Philia and eros love are feeling 'loves.' A person gets a good 'feeling' being around another person and continues the connection between the two people because of the good feelings. Agape love is not a 'feeling' love. Agape is a righteous, decisive, sacrificial, responsible, and unconditional love. Agape is the love Jesus gave to us by going to the cross. It was not a feeling love. He did have compassion, a feeling love for us too.

Satan has tricked us into believing we need to focus on the 'feeling' love in many church circles. This stops us from growing into the agape love and a deeper understanding of God. Agape love is a commitment to God, to righteousness, faith, hope, and obedience.

We have been led to believe Jesus saves you regardless of whether or not there are expectations by God - because Jesus loves you - period. As long as you are 'saved,' you do not need to live by God's expectations of righteousness and faith. The message preached is that we should sacrifice and serve one another but rarely conveys the message about making the right decisions, being righteous, or challenging our faith. The message becomes one of comfortability and complacency by believing you will be saved if you only love Jesus.

In Matthew 25, the ten virgins all had lamps but only five had extra oil. In order to have oil, a person would have to find the plant to make the oil, build a fire, boil the plant in the water, and extract the oil. There were other ways of extracting too. They all had lamps. We all have hearts that have been lit by the love of Jesus. Few of us are willing to take the time to make oil for our lamps because that takes work, time, and effort.

Righteousness and faith take effort to completely understand. We need to go through the fire from God and extract the good parts and throw away the waste in our lives. The five virgins that had the oil made it in to the banquet. The other five did not because they refused to make oil, not because they did not love the bride or groom.

Serving helps you refrain from making unrighteous decisions. What about when you are not serving? Righteousness and faith must be practiced and take precedence over everything. Also, if you serve but are not practicing righteousness and faith, your serving is done in vain and is hypocritical. God cares more about you being righteous than you serving someone. However, serving is supposed to increase your 'will' to be righteous. Your 'will' is connected to your beliefs and takes a decision to carry out, not a feeling of love.

If we look at Luke 6:46, the wise and foolish builders, Jesus says, "*...hears my words and put them into practice...they are like...*" Jesus talks about installing a foundation on rock or sand and the differences between them. Jesus is the cornerstone of the foundation – his love and commitment to us supports the building and opens the door to God for us.

What about the rest of the building? We always focus on Jesus being the foundation, but the rest of the building is left out. Jesus says to put his words into 'practice'. He does not say put words into a 'feeling.' Satan has turned this into experiencing the feeling of love and you are good with God because when you feel this feeling, this means you are close to God. This diet of Christians is causing starvation.

The walls of the building need to be built. The windows and doors need to be installed. The roof should be put on the house. Each room needs to be designed, where the kitchen is, the bathroom, the bedroom, living room, family room. Are you putting in carpet? Are you putting in dual pane windows to keep out the noise of the world? (Filtering what comes into your heart, mind, and soul) Are you installing a fireplace to keep it warm? (Serving the poor to soften your heart and feel the warmth of loving someone else) Are you installing a security system to protect against invaders? (Putting in place boundaries to stop allowing sin) How about running water to keep clean? (Confessing sin to others so they can pray for you) How about electricity to light the inside? (Keeping your heart bright by repenting of sin)

When we only focus on the foundation, we end up with a foundation and no building. Jesus is the foundation, specifically the cornerstone, and is the start of your walk with God. His love and your love for him become the cornerstone. You cannot become closer to God by feeling more. You can only work on constructing your building. Jesus opens the door for you to exercise righteousness and faith to build with. You would not just stand in a doorway your whole life; you enter through the door and into the building.

In my effort to walk as a Christian early on, I constantly tried to feel more love for God. How wrong I was about my love for God. If someone had separated my love for God from my ability to remain righteous, I would not have walked through the Valley of the Shadow of Death so many times. I should have been told I had a love for God, but what I needed to do is repent and make better decisions as a Christian and walk down the road to becoming more righteous. God loved me before I was a Christian, does so afterward as well, and never stops, but there are expectations.

As they say, what does not break you only makes you stronger. The funny part is that when I served and sacrificed, I was never told, "wow, your love for God is amazing." Serving and sacrificing is my duty as a Christian to show others I love them. Martha, in the Bible, was serving and sacrificing and Jesus told her Mary chose better.

I had a friend named Scott who helped me out immensely. He started to help me separate the difference between my love of God and the mistakes in my decision making. He simplified the chaos in my mind. My love for God was already there and God's love for me never stops. My decision-making stunk badly. He helped me to desire to be righteous and make better decisions at all costs. Getting advice from him and others was key in achieving a better decision-making process and percentage of righteousness. It also left my love for God and God's love for me in place, alive, and unchallenged.

In order to be more righteous, I also needed to be brutally open with my life. My friend Richard was given the task, by God, of building trust with me in order to be open with everything I was feeling and thinking, no matter what it was including all my sin. He was completely open with me, which made it easy for me to be open with him.

You see, the foundation of Jesus (love) was the basis for being able to construct a building of righteousness and faith thereby producing hope that I could become a man of integrity who God will consider worthy of living in heaven. The lie still exists in many groups, "Just believe and you will be saved."

My brother was introduced to church, which produced a fire for Jesus. The fire was soon put out by events that transpired in his life. He still believes in Jesus, but believes the myth that "just believing in God" is all it takes. There is no movement toward removing the sinful desires of his heart. He bought into the lie as many others have. If you are not removing sin, sin is removing you, from the kingdom. We are in a war trying to win the fight. God sees us as saints, so we need to behave as such – a new creation that desires to be righteous at all costs.

God had an expectation in the Old Testament that did not go away with the bringing forth of the New Testament. Jesus in the New Testament fulfilled the law of the Old Testament, but did not remove it. The expectations still exist to this day. The expectation to be righteous was then and is now. Jesus makes this pretty clear in several scriptures of the New Testament.

Acts 3:26 "When God raised up his servant, he sent him first to you to bless you by turning each of you *from your wicked ways*."
Matthew 23:26 "Blind Pharisee! First *clean the inside of the cup* and dish, and then the outside also will be clean."
Matthew 23:27 "Woe to you, teachers of the law and Pharisees, you hypocrites! You are like whitewashed tombs, which look beautiful on the outside but on *the inside are full of the bones of the dead and everything unclean*."
Luke 11:39 Then the Lord said to him, "Now then, you Pharisees clean the outside of the cup and dish, but inside *you are full of greed and wickedness*.
Matthew 5:20 "For I tell you that unless your righteousness *surpasses that of the Pharisees* and the teachers of the law, *you will certainly **not enter the kingdom** of heaven*."

The act of expecting righteousness rarely exists today. In order to be righteous, a person must know what it takes to be righteous. Churches teach that serving and sacrificing produces righteousness. This is a lie of Satan. People must be challenged to change their mind and heart, just like faith must be challenged in order to increase your faith. The funny thing is if you are not being and doing spiritual things, you are being and doing worldly things.

But, for some reason, challenging someone as a Christian brings with it a negative connotation. Preachers from the pulpit remove all challenges and only call people to love like Jesus; mostly because people do not like to or want to be challenged to be righteous. People who do not like to be challenged talk to preachers to have them remove the challenges from their preaching. These people use the belief that challenging is not loving as Jesus loved. This statement could not be further from the truth. In the preceding passages, Jesus challenged the Pharisees. We are not naturally righteous, faithful, loving, or hopeful. Deciding to be righteous is not easy.

In the book of 2 Timothy 3:16 it says, *"All Scripture is God-breathed and is useful for teaching, rebuking, correcting and training in righteousness..."* Teaching, rebuking, correcting, and training all require challenging a person to do things different and make righteous decisions. People must be challenged to get out of their comfort zone.

We are habitual in nature and doing things differently requires challenging yourself and denying your habitual nature to do whatever is not godly. Sadly, most will not challenge themselves to do anything but make it to church.

Being challenged is painful and sometimes brings suffering. We naturally want to believe we are right all the time and do not need to be challenged to change our mind or our hearts. We are smart enough to understand the word of God ourselves. We do not need anyone else telling us how to live our lives.

"I am saved by the blood of Christ anyway, so why do I need to work any harder. I cannot work my way in to heaven."

"God loves me as I am and do not need to change."

"God forgives me of all my sin now and in the future whether I change or not."

"As long as I believe in God, I am covered by the blood of Jesus to forgive sin."

"I will never remove all the sin out of my life, so I can just relax and do what I want because God loved me before I believed in him."

Excuses come in many sizes and shapes and all of them smell badly.

So….if Jesus is our example, then why does righteousness take a back seat to serving and sacrificing? Jesus was and is righteous. "Well, we are incapable of being completely righteous like Jesus, so we should only do what we are capable of doing." If this were a true statement, then people would not be accomplishing the impossible. We would still be looking at the moon wondering what it would be like to walk on the moon. Some people would still not be walking when they were told they would never walk again. They beat the odds because of their belief in the impossible.

Our beliefs move us to do the impossible. Love has the capability of moving us to do the impossible as well. Belief and love are powerful motivators. Someone believed we could travel to the moon. If the same person looked up and just realized his love for the moon, we probably would not have had someone walk on it.

Someone believed that an energy existed that could be used to make it to the moon; and the fuel was invented and used. If someone just loved the idea of an electrical energy that could be used to transform our lives and see at night, we would still be lighting candles. Belief moves people to action. Jesus believed he could save all people if he died on a cross. His belief was put into action while his love fueled his movements. Jesus said, "Not as I will, but as you will." This was not a feeling. It was commitment to God even at the cost of death.

If we believe we can continue to sin because God loves us, then Hebrew 10:26, *"If we deliberately keep on sinning after we have received the knowledge of the truth, no sacrifice for sins is left..."* is not true because God's love saves us no matter what and a portion of the Bible is untrue making the entire Bible worthless.

What is righteousness worth? If you remember, when atonement for sin was done in the Old Testament, God called it a pleasing aroma. Anyone who lacked faith usually died (When the spies came back from scoping out the Promised Land) or suffered from disease. Faith cannot be accompanied by unrighteousness and righteousness cannot be accompanied by a lack of faith.

Righteousness and faith go together. Being righteousness can be difficult. It is the reason why many people do not seek righteousness. Just a simple example of being given change for $20 when we gave $10 when purchasing a product is a challenge of whether or not we will be righteous and return the money that is not ours.

We need to set goals to achieve righteousness by removing sin. We need to be disciplined in our approach and aware of our circumstances. We also need to realize we will fail, but to get up and try again and reconcile our sin with God. We will always do something poorly in the beginning, and through training will become better.

We are lucky because God gives us a second chance when we realize we made a mistake. The horror of our own pathetic attempt at righteousness brings about a humbling experience. We ask forgiveness from God and learn from the mistake. Then humility has a chance to grow in our souls because we are not perfect. JOB was not perfect but was righteous.

Sin is unrighteousness. If we do not get in touch with our sin, as God made the Israelites do in the Old Testament, our hearts become hardened by sin's deceitfulness.

Marriage is a perfect example of how sin damages everything it touches. If sin exists in marriage, trust is broken. Sin then keeps piling on top of itself until both people cannot deal with it any longer and divorce takes place. If sin is dealt with, the marriage has a chance of continuing and growing stronger. Not one person married another because they hated that person to begin with.

Early in my marriage, my job consisted of contacting repair companies to help fix homes in homeowners associations and rentals I managed. I met a representative from a painting company who was a young female. We had lunch and discussed the company she worked with and the expectations I had of companies that worked with me. I asked the representative to come to a Bible discussion groups at our house. I told my wife about our meeting and that she was coming.

My wife had valid feelings of concern over me meeting alone with the young woman for lunch. I dismissed it, but my wife's feelings of distrust kept growing, of which I set the seed in place to do so. We finally sat down and talked through the situation. She poured out her feelings of distrust, and if allowed to grow, would have damaged our marriage. We prayed for God to remove the walls being built in our hearts. We also prayed for my responsibility in the situation of not protecting my wife's heart by placing the seeds of distrust in the first place. I did not make my wife's heart feel protected by being involved in situations where my heart could be tempted with the young woman.

We both were able to repent of our sin (change our heart and mind) since we got in touch with our sin. If my wife had not expressed her sin, the sin would have piled up and probably turned into something larger and uglier at some point. If I had not been open to hearing her sin, then there would be no communication between us to alleviate the wall and expose my sin. Ugliness would have resulted. I loved my wife with actions.

I have the 'feeling' of love for my wife. The feeling of love is very difficult to have when we are engaged in an intense argument. The feeling usually goes away. During those times, I have to practice commitment, righteousness, and faith. I have to make a decision about what my actions will be. This is the only way I will continue to believe everything will work out and we will make it through the conflict. If all I had to fall back on were love, our marriage would end up being just two people living together being horrible toward each other or the marriage would not exist at all.

When we are in touch with our sin and clean out our hearts of the sin that exists, we are free to live. I am talking about really living. When we are righteous, we have clarity of mind, heart, and soul. We are not supposed to feel we are only waiting for death. Jesus said we have life to the full while on earth. Feeling alive and free is an incredible feeling. We move from fear to confidence, hate to love, chaos to peace, and pride to humility. We try the impossible. Our faith increases. Our life becomes worth living.

On another note, in some church circles, they "bind up the devil." How do they know whether God allowed the devil into their life or the devil just came into their life itself? If the devil was sent by God to bring a testing of righteousness to that person, then if that person "bound up the devil," that person is rejecting testing, teaching, and training from God to make right choices.

Faith is increased when we are pressed into a corner by evil and call upon God to rescue us while we are making righteous decisions. We see God do miraculous things and this increases our faith. If we constantly "bind up the devil," then we will not have our faith grow leaning on God for our salvation. We come to believe we can do it ourselves which is opposite to what God wants – us to rely on him.

It is crazy to think we need bad circumstances for our faith or righteousness to be increased. But think about it. If everything was good and okay, as it was in the Garden of Eden, and as it is with many wealthy people, do we need to rely on God for anything. So, if you are binding up the devil, you may be as a rich person needing to go through the eye of a needle to be saved. Squelching God's intent for your life may be costing you life eternal itself.

The love syndrome causes us to believe love is all we need. However, it does not matter if we stand on one foot chanting excerpts from the Bible, speak in unintelligible words, hold our hands in the air, remove music within our congregation, move our hands in the sign of the cross in front of our face and heart, because these man made traditions have no meaning in the fight to be righteous.

Learning to love is not the most important aspect of our walk because it is the beginning of our building. Righteousness must be practiced to exist in our souls. Galatians 5:13 expresses the chapter in a nice neat little ball, *"you, my brothers and sisters, were called to be free. But do not use your freedom to indulge the flesh* (unrighteousness)" We become free from sin by deciding to practice righteousness; and this is our worship of God. Singing songs, serving, and loving one another with clean hearts, minds, and souls is an aroma pleasing to God.

Not Forsaken

"A despairing man should have the devotion of his friends even though he forsakes the fear of the Almighty. But my friends are undependable..." (JOB 6:14)

Let us face it, people get desperate at times. Anyone in desperation becomes very needy, but for what. Homeless people are desperate for food. People losing their homes are desperate for help. JOB despaired for an answer from God. Despair causes people to respond not always in the ways we expect them to. JOB's response becomes difficult to comprehend because he tells his friends he stopped fearing the Almighty. On top of that, JOB tells them to still have devotion toward him even though he stopped fearing the Almighty. Sounds like an arrogant request.

I have had friends who walked away from God, or stopped fearing God, and turned to their own ways again only to turn to me and say they are no different than before (they were) – that our friendship remains the same (but it did not).

To have the same devotion toward them as when they were walking as a Christian is not easy. I still communicate occasionally, but I do not seek out their friendship as I used to when they were practicing godliness. I ask myself the question of whether they were despairing or in sin when they left. Most of the time it was sin that separated them from God. Still, I was undependable in my friendship toward them.

People go through tough times and give up on God. It is not easy to believe in something you cannot see. This is why God must reveal himself to us on a constant basis. If we are not looking for how god reveals himself in our lives, we miss the confirmation that God exists and is working. Our beliefs will change, and we stop fearing God and live our lives without seeking God.

I have been in despair repeatedly. While in my despair, I have been hammered by my friends. They tell me to get right with God by confessing, and to clarify, my despair is usually from sin. At times, I despaired because of some simple things such as a will I be fired from my job, actually needing work, or sin of some sort. Of course, if we believe we have the power to make a decision not to despair, we should be able to get out of despair. This is more easily said than done.

In my despair, I turn toward sin many times. Sin causes me to despair more. In JOB's despair, he does not turn toward sin, get drunk, curse, or get angry with God. JOB attacks God's creative purpose contained in Genesis 1. He curses the light, the light of the day he was born, the day he was born, time, and purpose of his life. I believe this is very personal with God because God is the creator. However, the incredible part is God listens to JOB.

God's answer at the end of the book of JOB addresses JOB personally on the points of creation JOB expressed. God's speech is framed from the standpoint of being the Creator and JOB is the created. God exposes their relationship for JOB to figure out and come to grips with. Even though God was quiet, he was still with JOB, listening, as he is with us. Since JOB was righteous through the whole experience, God only addressed the Creator and created points expressed by JOB.

JOB must have been comforted by God's words at the end of the chapter reconfirming his relational place with God as well as knowing that God did not abandon him. Also, God at the end literally says, "Good JOB, but your friends need to sacrifice for they were not quite right."

Still, some are still wondering why God did not offer compassion at the end of the chapter. We want to believe that when someone is in pain he or she requires compassion.

An idea has been stimulated through our society that those with limitations are different from us and should be treated as different and given special privileges. I look at people in wheel chairs and feel compassion for them because they are not like me – standing and able to get around easily. Carlos Mencia, a comedian, changed my mind about this concept. He was at an amusement park when a person in a wheel chair was brought in front of him to board a ride before Carlos.

Carlos stood up to try and stop what was happening because he believed what was happening was wrong. Carlos pointed out that people with limitations do not want to be treated different from people without limitations. They wanted to be considered as equal more than anything. The person in the wheel chair with limitations agreed with Carlos. Everyone wants to be treated as equals. With God, we are unequal though and the expectation of compassion from him comes through Christ.

We do need to have compassion in certain situations people find themselves. Compassion says, "We cannot feel what you feel, but are here for you to meet your needs in any way we can. We also say we care."

When my kids experience pain, my heart goes out to them. I do everything I can to be there for them. Although, every little bit of pain does not require I am compassionate. My son has gotten a small cut on his finger and wants me to be compassionate, which I have to refuse because the level of the damage is very minimal. If I were to be compassionate at every instance of pain, he will become a hypochondriac because I am reinforcing his belief that all pain is of high importance.

God knows when to give compassion and when not to give compassion. Our time on this earth is but a mist, as soon as you see it, it disappears. The pain we experience is temporary even though it seems like it will never go away. When we die, the pain goes away, according to God.

During our time on earth, God is always there for us, but he does not always offer compassion because if he did, we would never strengthen our hearts, minds, and souls. Remember, God puts us through the fire to refine us. If he gave us compassion all the time, we would never go through the fire and his creation would never strengthen, impurities would not be removed, and we would not have faith worth more than gold.

If we were to always have compassion for our children for every little bit of pain they experience, we will stop them from maturing and being refined by the fire. We may be stopping God's purpose in their life. Standing in the way of God's purpose for our children is like saying, "God, I know better than you do. My child needs compassion."

God was there for JOB, but he did not step in to comfort JOB. God is no different for us. We need to go through the fire, which is not easy.

I had to go through the fire of making it through college. I had to go through the fire of losing my father to emphysema of the lungs. I had to go through the fire of breaking an ankle to slap me back into exercising again. I had to go through the fire of attempting to build a business and losing everything I put into it only to see that my marriage needed help; and I was the problem.

I need to go through the fire because I see how my character changes when making it to the other side. This is true love from God. I do not expect compassion from God when going through the fire, but I do know he is listening while I am experiencing the fire. While in the fire, God expects me to make righteous decisions. When I fail to make the righteous decision, he puts me back through the fire until I decide right. He is the potter. I am the clay.

The most interesting part about JOB's journey is that JOB never asked God to take away the pain. Everyone I know desires not to experience pain including myself. We also pray to take the pain away from those we know. There is a pill for just about every kind of pain. Isn't the pain we experience actually the fire from God trying to transform our lives to be righteous and holy? I try not to ask God to take the pain away anymore. I ask God to show me the way out. Pain is inevitable and a necessary part of life.

When we know others are experiencing pain in their life, we see it as negative. We should be praying for the individual experiencing the pain to make righteous decisions during their trials and to learn the lesson – not to take the pain away. We should pray for the person to see the path God wants them to take and see God reveal himself.

Why should we stand in the way of God's purpose for their life? God is allowing their pain for a reason – and that is because their faith is worth more than gold. God is transforming them right before our eyes. Do we even notice the transformation? Yes, we should have compassion for them, but be excited to see what the final product is going to be. What is the wisdom gained from their refinement experience?

Another belief we have is to pray that God is there with the individual experiencing pain. Has God left? Does God not know about the pain or care about them? God's heart goes out to all of us, is always there for us, never leaves us, and he always desires our hearts. God loves us so much he sent his son to die for us. Why do we pray for God to be with those in pain? To me these are useless prayers.

Useless prayers are prayed because people cannot think of anything else to pray. Much less, our own heart is not really connected to those in pain when we pray useless prayers. We should pray they see God more clearly.

Useless prayers permeate our prayer time mainly because we are not saying anything of importance. Prayers come out with no real substance. Praying is supposed to provoke God to answer, confirm he is listening, tell God we are grateful, recognize his supremeness, help us fight temptation; give us our daily needs, and more. Becoming accustomed to praying useless prayers lessens the power of prayer and God acting for them. God does not know what to do with weak prayers. Our faith needs to be such that when we pray, we pray healthy and strong prayers so God can act. Prayer is powerful and we should be careful what we pray about.

What if I came to my friend and said the same thing every time we got together. "Hi Doug, our father who art in heaven, hallowed be thy name…" "Hi Doug, our father who art in heaven, hallowed be thy name…." What kind of friend would I have over time? Our prayers need to mean something and have purpose for God and people. Because the word "amen" means "so be it," all the more important for meaning to be attached to prayers.

But you say, "oh no, my prayers weren't answered. God was not listening." "I do not need a God who does not listen and respond." Fortunately, you do not know everything and God does. He knows whether answering your prayers is in the best interest of everyone involved within your prayers. God has a better view from where he is sitting and ultimately knows the right decision to make in the best interest of people. Let us not be arrogant to think our prayers are what is right. We cannot see the whole picture.

My family members that are not Christians are very important to me. I want so much for them to commit themselves to living as disciples practicing righteousness. My heart felt a deep emotional desire for them one day, and I prayed for God to do whatever he needed to do to bring them to him. Of course, God has more desire for my family than I do, but I still felt a need to pray with everything I had in my soul. A couple days later, one of my family members came close to death. God tried to get their attention. It spurred movement toward God, but that soon died. Still, I desire to be in heaven with them.

My wife and I used to live in an area where very large trees were planted in front of each house for a whole block. The trees had been growing for 50 years and were the home for about 1000 black crows. Every morning we would be awakened around 5:30am because of the loud obnoxious sound the birds were making in the trees along our block. I was more of a night person, so waking at 5:30 was not my idea of starting out my day right. This went on for a couple of years and it seemed more crows showed up each year because it was a big party in those trees and the sound got louder as time went by.

One morning, I had had enough. I woke up and out of desperation prayed a very emotional and intense prayer for God do something with those crows making all the noise. I begged him to help us live in peace. I loved our house and did not want to move.

A couple of weeks after I prayed my intense prayer, the West Nile Virus came and killed most of the crows. Crows were laying everywhere, and there were only a few left in the trees. I was overjoyed to have the silence, but yet sorrowful for the crows. I realized the power of prayer in that moment.

How do we fight this feeling of abandonment? First, we need to understand God is incapable of abandoning us. Even to those in the Old Testament making decision against God were never abandoned. Their lives just took a completely different path away from God rather than toward him.

For instance, Achin's sin of taking a few of the things that belonged to God; God never left him. God was still there. God knew exactly what he did. Unfortunately, Achin and his family were killed because of their unrighteousness and disobedience over a gold cup and robe. They did not take God seriously. They refused to acknowledge the desires of God.

Throughout the stories in the Old Testament, God is continuously trying to get people to understand he is serious about what he wants done. Obedience in order to be righteous is the message.

I turn to the story where the Ark of the Covenant was being carried along and one of the carriers tripped while carrying it. The Ark of the Covenant started to fall. A person standing on one side of the Ark of the Covenant saw it was falling, reached over to help straighten it up to prevent it from falling. He died instantly. God was displaying his seriousness of being obedient. The Ark was never to be touched unless God allowed someone to touch it. Even though the person was trying to save the Ark of the Covenant, he disobeyed and died for it. Yes, it is confusing to our little finite brains. Just accept God is serious about his intentions.

As Christians, we lose sight of the seriousness of God because "love" gets in the way. We cannot believe that anyone should be "really serious" if they love someone. If God is the same now as he was thousands of years ago, and is never changing, his "seriousness" still exists. He is serious about obedience, righteousness, and love, not just having a feel good love.

Fortunately, God gave us marriage relationships to help us understand "seriousness" on a completely different level than we are used to understanding as an unmarried person.

When I was single, I was not too serious about anything. I was interested in having fun and enjoying life without the burdens of too much seriousness. I was serious about having fun though. When I married my wife, my life changed dramatically. I had to get serious on about 90 percent of my life. Life was still fun, but it was more seriousness than fun.

The major issue I learned was that my actions had serious consequences for my wife. My actions affected her in ways unknown to me before I became married. This "seriousness" started infiltrating every aspect of my life. I started analyzing who I was before God and who I was before her. Up to that point, I was just who I was and did not think much about it. I also started thinking about who I wanted to be; and how I wanted people to perceive me. As I started moving toward who I wanted to be for God, my wife, and myself, I made some good and horrible decisions along the way.

I started seeing the seriousness of God contained in the Old Testament and New. If I was going to be like Jesus, I needed to consider the seriousness at which he approached people and issues. God is serious about sin. Needless to say, I have worked hard on removing sin and atoning for the sin I commit. The sins contained in Galatians 5 are a good start, but I needed to get to the deeper sins of pride and selfishness.

I did not know how deep those rivers flowed until I started trying to stop the river. I started to build the dam across the river from one side, and the other side of the river erodes away making it seem impossible to contain the flow of sin. Still, I press on to take the prize.

Pride stops us from removing that feeling of abandonment by God. We tell ourselves, "I am smart enough. I do not need God for every single thing in my life. I can do this!" Proverbs rings true then. Pride comes before a fall. What happens when we fall? We experience pain of some sort.

We will not get away from feeling abandonment, pain, despair, and lack of fear for God at times in our life. We need to understand that God is serious and never leaves us. We can turn to love as a motivator out of our feeling of despair and abandonment.

This is what makes the Christian walk a rather sea-tossed, earthquake shaken, tornado blown experience like no other experience in life. Well worth it though. The good thing is we are never abandoned by God no matter how rough it gets.

The Most Righteous Person

First, I want to express that God's grace is what saves us. We cannot earn our salvation. We do need to work on our walk with God as a disciple though and that takes effort.

JOB was a man who was blameless and upright, feared God, and shunned evil. What kind of man was this? Is there anyone on earth that you would put that much faith and belief in to be the most righteous person alive? What does blameless mean? What does upright mean? These are the questions I have.

I realize that Jesus came to forgive sins and we have that forgiveness now. What about then? What about the time JOB was walking the earth? How was someone able to do this? How could someone be blameless? How could someone be upright?

We know through understanding the life of Jesus, the meaning of the cross, and the forgiveness Jesus gave to the people who beat him and nailed him to the cross that we can be righteous too, sprinkled with love.

After Jesus went through the cross, did life change with regard to righteousness? JOB did have the luxury of knowing Jesus because he had an intimate relationship with God. JOB was blameless and upright without the sacrifice of Jesus. Now we have the knowledge of knowing love through Jesus in order to be righteous and upright.

According to Dictionary.com, blameless means – free from or not deserving blame; guiltless. God believes JOB is guilt free and does not deserve any blame for anything. He has kept his life from being guilty of some act or word or deed. To be completely guilt free would be an amazing feeling.

I have past guilt that peeks its head up every occasionally that bothers me. I regret not doing the right thing during those times. However, we are guilt free in Christ through his blood and sacrifice that moves our hearts to make the right decisions. Still, the guilt shows up at times to yell at me.

Upright means – vertical or erect and honest, honorable or just. God considered JOB honorable and just. JOB could hold his head up high and walk with confidence. Walking with his head up and being humble at the same time gives an opposing vision to me.

I envision being humble as a person having his head bowed down in submission. If you are honorable, you can hold your head up and face people with confidence. You are supposed to be able to do the same thing being humble, but I am conflicted. The conflict I will have to work out myself.

JOB not only thought of himself, but thought of others too. He offered sacrifices for sin not only for himself but others too. Maintaining integrity and uprightness took sacrificing for sin then and the same does now. He made sure he was capable of helping others by shunning evil and atoning for sin.

When all the destruction took place with his family and herds, what type of man would say, *"the Lord gave and the Lord took away. May the name of the Lord be praised."* I do not know anyone living today who would have that same spirit. Most people get depressed over simple things such as their car breaking down.

I have heard stories of very wealthy people losing everything only to commit suicide. God praised JOB saying he maintained his integrity and there is no one like him.

How great would it be if God felt the same way with us? How would you feel if you knew God felt this way about you? We want to know that God feels the same way. All you have to do is offer sacrifices and refrain from sin. We have the sacrifice and that is Jesus. Do you refrain from sin?

In the Old Testament, people had to offer sacrifices for their sin. I am not going into the differences between the Old Testament and New Testament with regard to sacrifices and atonement. It is an interesting subject, but I will leave it at that because it is not the focal point of this book.

With Jesus dying on a cross, sacrifices have been offered for you and you need to refrain from sin. Therefore, if I am reading this right, all we need to do is refrain from sin to be upright and have integrity. If we do sin, we look to Jesus' sacrifice for clearance of our sin. We then are considered by God to be upright and have integrity. Simple, right? Not at all.

Sin entangles us, grabs us, and holds on to us with all of its might and strength. Sin causes us to think differently, feel differently, and make stupid decisions. Sin can make us walk from the truth, leave the love of God, and choose to live without him even after we have tasted the sweetness God offers. We have to be on constant alert to the deceptions of sin.

Some say if you are truly with God, there is no way to walk away. King Saul was a man who walked with God and walked away. King David walked away but was slapped back to an understanding by Nathan the Prophet.

Guilty of sin, we hang our heads in shame reflecting on the stupid things we have done and we believe we are disqualified. Yes! We have disqualified ourselves from Heaven because of our own evilness unless we repent. God's law points a condemning finger at us and shouts: "*the soul that sins shall surely die*" and off we march to the death chambers.

Luckily, we have Jesus to tell us we are forgiven when we repent, but we have to ask for it. JOB obviously kept a really sin free life somehow without the knowledge of the death of Jesus' on a cross.

Who is this person, JOB, superman? Did he come from another planet? How does someone live a life like this? What would his life look like?

I watched this show on TV where the host travelled around the globe looking for super humans or humans that had very unique talents, strengths, or aspects that set them apart from every other human on the planet. Stan Lee, an author of comics, produced the show trying to find those unique individuals. There were several people with various talents that were unexplainable. One guy could hit a bullet with a sword; another guy would eat glass, and so on.

One man lived in India and could take electricity in the amount of about 240 volts with a level of amperage enough to severely injure a normal person. He had tried to kill himself one day by throwing himself across some electrical lines. He did not die from the electricity but realized he had something that made him resistant to the electrical current.

He started putting on shows where he would plug himself between a wall outlet and a toaster or other device such as a hot plate and show he could take incredible amounts of electricity. Even though these super humans, as they were named on the show, could do incredible things, understanding how JOB lived is even more astounding.

I look at JOB's heart and feel JOB was a super human because of his sacrifices. I cannot ignore his heart to please God. His desire for his children to be righteous is an example all of us should take note too. I certainly do not think this way and have been making an effort to do so. Most of us just worry about ourselves.

Thinking a little more about JOB's children, we see some good teachings within the sacrifices he made. Instead of disciplining our children with the rod all the time, as they get older, I need to turn them toward God to pray and receive his forgiveness when they sin. I need to pray with them asking God's forgiveness for their misdeeds and character faults. This act points their hearts toward God and the reconciliation that is necessary as they live life. I cannot count how many times I have done this reconciliation for myself. My children need to learn this too.

When our children study the Bible and finally come to an understanding of their sin, confess with their mouths, are cut to the heart by understanding what Jesus did for them on the cross, they will start to build faith in God and go through the act of praying for their sins and the sins of others and their children. The actions taken will make more sense to them as they come to a relationship with God.

I believe one of the main ingredients for JOB's righteousness was the intimate relationship he had with God (JOB 29:4) that blessed him. The God who created everything has a line of communication with JOB to an intimate level. God knew the intimate and vulnerable areas of JOB's life. JOB had to know God's thoughts as well.

Intimacy is a two-way street. A person cannot be intimate by himself or herself, although many of us think we can. Many Christians believe all they have to do is believe in Jesus and listen to the preacher on Sundays living without intimacy with God. Studying the Bible does not come into the picture as a piece of the puzzle when communicating with God either.

Learning and understanding God takes studying the Bible every day to know who God is, what he expects, what is his character, and find the intimacy on a deep level. Then we can imitate the character of Jesus more accurately. I would conclude JOB had a good idea of God's character through his intimacy and communication even though there was confusion as to what was happening to him at the time.

JOB offered the sacrifices necessary for the forgiveness of sins and had a character that far exceeded the human character today? In JOB 31:1, JOB says he made a covenant with his eyes not to look lustfully at a young woman. He goes on to say in 31:9 he has not been enticed by a woman. This covenant to shun lustful sin shows his willingness to be completely pure in mind, thought, and heart. How many of us are willing to do that? How many of us do not look at woman lustfully? This includes the scenarios we make up in our mind about females we come across.

Scenarios in our minds run the course of the initial meeting to the final act of enjoyment over our achievement and the feelings of pleasure gained. The Bible says to take every thought captive and that means the scenarios we create.

In JOB's pursuit of righteousness, he not only pursued it for his family, but also 'broke the fangs of the wicked' (JOB 29:17).

We have a justice system consisting of police, detectives, lawyers, and judges that are supposed to confront the wicked. Unfortunately, the corruption within those organizations is every bit as prevalent as other organizations.

The level of corruption in corporations has increased throughout the years destroying millions of lives. Fortunately, those who actually fight for truth, righteousness, and justice are among the corrupt trying to make a difference by exposing their schemes. JOB was one of those people. Being a Christian means, we need to do the same.

We learn in church to overlook corruption because we should love people instead. Yes, there is corruption in church too. This is because there are people in church who are not perfect. There is selfish gain, pride, arrogance, un-openness to being disciplined, and a myriad of other sins that permeate the church. However, we are taught to overlook them and not confront them because it is unloving. JOB is an example of what we need to be accepting or not accepting from everything around us.

JOB not only broke the fangs of the wicked, but also did not 'gloat' over winning. A powerful and yet similar heart to Jesus is expressed in JOB 31:29. *"If I have rejoiced at my enemy's misfortune or gloated over the trouble that came to him - I have not allowed my mouth to sin by invoking a curse against their life..."* JOB did not hate his enemies and did not express joy when they experienced trouble or defeat. Jesus is similar in that he says do not hate your enemies, but goes deeper saying to pray for them, give them the shirt off your back, and walk the extra mile with them and love them.

What is the purpose of praying for our enemies? Our hatred toward people is not righteous. Praying clears our heart and mind to see the schemes of the enemy. Hatred blinds our hearts and can explode into bitterness or an even more damaging trait. Hatred toward an enemy is a red flag waving from a rooftop of our hearts. When we hate an enemy, there is no possible way to win their hearts or even understand why the hate in the first place. Praying for them makes us realize we are no different from them in our need for God. God did not say we should not confront them on their dirty deeds; just that we need to be careful in doing so or be caught up in sin ourselves.

Even today, as we have Jesus to call upon to rescue us from this dark world, living for God is a difficult task because we can be hated. There are times when we do well and are satisfied with our relationship. We feel good, and then there are times when we are walking through the desert looking at all the bones around us feeling forgotten or separated because of the sin that so easily entangles us. Being the hated is not fun.

It can be said that JOB had a much easier lifestyle without all the advertisements wanting to make us to do one thing or another, to stay up with the Jones's, or to wreak havoc in our mental state of mind by various means and methods.

The amount of information that travels through our minds nowadays is astounding. How is it that anyone copes with the stress of living today? JOB certainly did not have to deal with the amount of stimulation that we have in society today.

Was life easier to live during that time? Maybe a little. Other things caused stress. Marauders, disease in animals and people, weather damaging crops, are just a few of the stresses. Many of us do not consider those things because they do not affect our lives now. We have exchanged the stress of marauders for the stress of driving a car.

This is the reason why we need to be walking with Jesus even more than any other time in the past. Straying from the path and walking completely in the dark can be a daily or hourly pendulum going from the dark and back into the light until we are strengthened.

The mind is clouded from the bombardment of stimulation in the effort to take our minds off what is true and real. Our main drive is to remain holy through all the exposure. Every sin is so easy nowadays that it becomes a fight every minute to stay free from the entanglement.

The answer to being holy is found in the New Testament, which is more of a commandment: "*You MUST be PERFECT as your Heavenly Father is perfect.*" Obviously, "perfection" cannot be improved upon, but let us zero in on that fact that the Messiah, Jesus, tells us it MUST be done! Another statement by Jesus says that we must be more righteous than the Pharisees. I guess we can throw out the idea that just believing in God is enough to get you to heaven then. It is an absolute confirmation of the ludicrousness of "just believing."

What we need to look at here is the relationship that JOB had with God. He had an intimate relationship that made him guilt free, blameless, upright, honorable, just, full of integrity, and righteous before God. Jesus brings you into that relationship through love.

When we have an intimate relationship with God through Jesus by studying the Bible and allowing God to speak to us through his word, we become righteous and holy. This means understanding the sacrifices given for our life through Jesus just like JOB sacrificed for his children, Jesus sacrificed for his children, in whom we are.

We must repent and turn from our sin, receive forgiveness, and change our lifestyle in order to be holy. We have daily work to do with ourselves and work to do with others. Unfortunately, some churches believe people must be controlled so they do not sin.

Many organizations make up man made laws, regulations, or policies to stop people from sinning. These include a variety of rules from "if you are Christian, you cannot dance," "music is not allowed in church," "Christians do not go to the movies because this supports the satanic movie industry," "Dancing is not allowed at weddings," etc. You get the point.

Jesus came to give us freedom – not to burden us with chains right after he has broken them off our souls. The Talmud did this for the Jews by inflicting all kinds of laws too. This is the controlling nature of people to have power over other people "in their best interests" which equates to burdening people instead of freeing them from the burdens. Jesus told this to the Pharisees of his day as well. They were burdening people instead of leading them into righteousness and obedience of God's laws.

Of course, some of the rules made by man can actually be thought of as good to follow. If they are impressed upon people to follow or else, they become burdens – the exact thing Jesus came to rid us of. The desire to be righteous should be cultivated not controlling people to make sure they make the right decisions.

An example would be dancing. I had a friend who went to a church where dancing was not allowed. He was a music major and loved dancing and music. The church believed dancing could lead to dropping the guard against sexual sin and produce a decision to sin. Making a rule, law, or regulation to prohibit dancing is not the way to go. Creating a heart to desire to be righteous at all costs is better. This heart will put in stoppers to refrain from the act. The heart becomes exercised in righteousness because the heart desires to be righteous not because someone was told to do it. We usually rebel over laws at some point anyway.

When those people are out in other areas of life and the heart has not been disciplined into desiring righteousness, the rules take a back seat and become invalid because in our hearts, we do not want to live by rules. The effect is devastating. The lack of "desire" to follow God's laws and heart disappears while away from the church.

Teaching conviction about what dancing would lead to is far better because if the dancers decide to sin, they can repent and seek to gain a deeper conviction by their openness of confession. Humility is a byproduct of confession. They learn to take responsibility for their sin because ultimately, they alone will stand before God to take responsibility for their life. Preachers will not be standing next to them in heaven telling them what to say or do or how to act. Their heart has not been exercised in righteousness. People need to gain their own convictions about what holiness, righteousness, uprightness, integrity, and honor consists of through their own failures.

What we need to understand is that we cannot force people to be righteous in order to get people to heaven. God did not force us either. People must get themselves there by their own desire to be righteous. All we can do is try to move their hearts to do the things that will get them to heaven. We need to equip people to desire righteousness. We cannot force someone through regulations and legalism. Those man made laws, policies, and regulations do nothing for any individual in the effort to get them to heaven.

People must realize they are responsible to get themselves to heaven and to exercise their heart to get there. People must help each other and be open to being helped to learn to become responsible and stay responsible for their own salvation. Trying to control people's actions through petty policies, laws, and regulations is opposite to what Jesus teaches. People are not God. I think that it was what Paul eluded to when he said run and finish the race – self-discipline. (1 Cor 9:24)

But, you say there are laws of the land we follow such as traffic laws that are good. Man implements laws to control society's actions so we can come to a "standard" of understanding. This way we can live more peacefully with each other. Those laws do not produce a "desire" to be righteous, have integrity, honesty, etc. They are an act of controlling people only. If we do not follow the laws, then we have the possibility of being fined or going to jail.

The same can be true in churches who disallow dancing or ear piercings. God never said we "had" to follow his laws. God said, "Please follow my laws because they are good for your soul." Sure, there is the penalty for not following the laws or accepting Jesus' love, which God administers, not people. Even being God, who brings justice, does not make us follow his laws. We must desire to follow them to become righteous and holy.

Creating the desire in someone to be righteous and holy is a difficult task. Our own lives become the example of demonstrating to people that you practice righteousness in your household. The fact is, studying the Bible and seeking an understanding and relationship with God should increase your desire to be righteous and holy; it does not always happen that way. Man's laws, rules, regulations, and policies do not increase desire. Faith, hope and love anchor the heart, soul, and mind and a decision has to be made to practice righteousness in order to be holy, and when cultivated, is more powerful than laws of any kind.

JOB was righteous, upright, and blessed, not because he was perfect, but because God had had a relationship with him and desired to give him the blessing for his righteousness. JOB had an intense desire for God too. JOB obeyed the laws, but much more than that was his heart to be righteous and upright for himself and his family. This is what God delighted in.

God did not delight in JOB following the laws but JOB's desire and decision to be holy. Our desire to be holy delights God, and not because we did not dance at weddings, removed earrings, or refrained from going to movies. If you cannot equip people to desire to be righteous, then all you are left with is controlling others or just teaching that legalism is the answer. Jesus did not control us, but wanted us to desire to love him as he loved us, respond to is call, and to desire to be righteous and holy.

The Rich Young Ruler

I play soccer twice a week with a bunch of people who enjoy the game as much as I do. Each game is different from other games played because we do not pick teams. We just split up into darks and lights and play. The players I play with are excellent players, and their skill level is very high compared to my level of skill.

An unusual phenomenon occurs on the field though. We do not keep score, but we know instinctively who is winning. Occasionally, an overbalance of good players ends up on one side. The opposing side with less skill level is usually beaten badly because of the comparison of skill levels. However, the team with the less skill level, on occasion, ends up beating the team with the overwhelming number of good players. How does that happen? I am not sure, but when I have been on the lesser-skilled team during those times, the mental connection of the players to each other is tremendous. It is as if each player knows where the other one is going to be and passes the ball in that direction to make the play and score.

This sense of intuitiveness, or whatever you want to call it, is the driving force for the team to score goals and win. You just know the rightness of the strategy of play when it happens. The sense of knowing is powerful.

When leaders talk about certain passages in the Bible, it is hard to get a sense of a complete picture regarding the passage. The sermon paints a partial picture with pieces missing that leaves a person with a void to fill. Not knowing what that void is causes us to walk away with an unsettled feeling.

One such passage when spoken about has bothered me for many years. The passage is the rich young ruler. The story is located in Luke 18:18, Mark 10:17, and Matthew

19:16. I have always believed a deeper meaning existed to the passage but was missing when anyone talks about it. Yes, some of the meaning brought out of the scripture does make sense, but I felt it just touched the surface. And I felt unsettled.

THE RICH YOUNG RULER
A certain ruler asked him, "Good teacher, what must I do to inherit eternal life?"
"Why do you call me good?" Jesus answered. "No one is good—except God alone. You know the commandments: 'You shall not commit adultery, you shall not murder, you shall not steal, you shall not give false testimony, honor your father and mother.'"
"All these I have kept since I was a boy," he said.
When Jesus heard this, he said to him, "You still lack one thing. Sell everything you have and give to the poor, and you will have treasure in heaven. Then come, follow me."
When he heard this, he became very sad, because he was very wealthy.
Jesus looked at him and said, "How hard it is for the rich to enter the kingdom of God! 25 Indeed, it is easier for a camel to go through the eye of a needle than for someone who is rich to enter the kingdom of God."
Those who heard this asked, "Who then can be saved?" Jesus replied, "What is impossible with man is possible with God."
Peter said to him, "We have left all we had to follow you!"
"Truly I tell you," Jesus said to them, "no one who has left home or wife or brothers or sisters or parents or children for the sake of the kingdom of God will fail to receive many times as much in this age, and in the age to come eternal life."

When Jesus was walking on the earth, he was considered a prophet by many, and not the Christ to come. People did not follow prophets but asked them to perform miracles. If the Christ was to come, though, how were they to react? What would people say? I certainly would be confused as to what to do or say around the Christ, especially during that time. What would make me believe he was the Christ?

If God controls everything, then either God blesses or he does not bless. Colossians 1:16 says, *"For in him all things were created: things in heaven and on earth, visible and invisible, whether thrones or powers or rulers or authorities; all things have been created through him and for him."* So, if this were true, then why would God bless someone to have riches only to make it difficult for them to enter the kingdom of God? Of course, this means "possibly" enter because all things are possible with God. Rich people are more than likely not going to enter the kingdom of God because "it is more difficult for a camel to go through the eye of a needle than a rich man to enter heaven."

Many people twist the meaning to mean that to have a Godly life is "to get rid of your monetary blessings" God gave you while in obedience to the law. You do not want to become rich lest you be counted out of the blessing of entering the kingdom of God.

This is the confusion I have been embroiled in for years. God blesses you, but do not take it because you might go to hell for it. Some say you have to have the right heart about your money, but Jesus says it is hard for the rich to enter the kingdom. He does not say it is what you do with your wealth that counts, well except to give it away.

Another strange part of the passage is we would expect Jesus to say, "Believe in me." Instead, he says, "Keep the commandments." Why didn't Jesus just say, "Believe in me?" Why did Jesus specifically say he needed to obey the law if the law was not important?

Next, Jesus says, you lack one thing. Was that one thing he lacked love? The ruler obeyed the law and was righteous but did not have love? In order to have love, you must give up everything.

To lack one thing would be incredible. I believe we all lack more than one thing. What did Jesus point out? Jesus did not say that following the laws was being legalistic. Jesus did not say all the ruler had to do was love him. Jesus did not want the ruler to throw out the law either. Just because you practice righteousness does not mean you love, however. Just because you practice love does not mean you have righteousness. Jesus drew a clear line for the ruler.

Let us look at a couple of other interpretations. A common interpretation is that Jesus was showing this person his sin. Jesus seemed to say he would be saved by keeping the commandments when he said, "did you keep the commandments." The interpretation states had he not kept the commandments, Jesus would then say he must be saved another way and that is "by faith in me." For me, this is borderline, almost there, but not quite all the way to the truth. Yes, having faith in Jesus is part of the big puzzle, but only part of that passage. Hope, faith, and love are the three friends that pal around together, not separately. We are also saved by grace through faith (Ephesians 2:8-9), not faith alone.

Other interpretations include the rich person asking, "What must I do to have it," which is a works mentality for the idea of salvation. The rich person was a law keeper and that alone does not ensure entrance to the kingdom of God. We all hold on to things that will keep us from fully following God though. We eventually change with God's help and get rid of those things, but we will never be perfect. We will always have something we are wrestling with until the day we leave this earth. We will always be "working" on something. We will always be "adhering to laws" of God and authorities. Although, these are good ideas, I do not feel this encompasses the true depth and nature of the scripture.

The passage of the rich young ruler goes to the very core or our humanity. That core stems from belief. What are your beliefs? Everyone has beliefs about everything in life. Beliefs can change as we grow up either by outside intervention or inside meditation. What was the rich young ruler's belief? He had some very strong beliefs and was confident in them.

The rich young ruler believed in God and followed the Law of Moses. He felt he was doing everything God had commanded of him. Jesus did not say otherwise. He kept the law since he was a young boy, and Jesus respected him for his belief. Obviously, the ruler had character, integrity, honor, so much so that Jesus told him he lacked only one thing.

The evidence the ruler was following all the laws was that he became wealthy and God had blessed him for it. This type of thinking is prevalent in Jewish and Christian circles. God does want to prosper us. This was true with JOB's friends as well. Follow God and you will be taken care of and live well and more than likely become wealthy because of it.

The laws of God are good to live life by because they assure good business between people and companies. They bring honor, respect, integrity, character; talents are used correctly, this being the very ethical nature of business to increase business income.

It is a fact businesses that practice unethical values will cause other businesses to be less likely to do business with them again. When good biblical values are practiced, there is an advantage over not so ethical businesses. This is not to say that when businesses increase in size and income that people are not swayed to the dark side and lose their values. It happens all the time. However, to increase in business, you need to have good values and ethics to get there. People must trust in the business.

The rich young ruler has been confirmed in his belief through his wealth and keeping the commandments that he has been following what God desires of people. What does Jesus do? Jesus targets the rich young ruler's belief. Jesus gets to the core of what he believes and asks, "Do you believe I am just a prophet, or am I who I say I am, God in the flesh, the Christ? If you believe I am God in the flesh, then you just spoke to God and I am telling you the truth. I want you to break your man made beliefs, and receive godly beliefs and follow me. There is something much bigger here that you will understand only by giving up everything. Is it worth the loss to you?"

Luke 14:33 says, *"In the same way, those of you who do not give up everything you have cannot be my disciples."* Jesus asked him to break his belief about prosperity equaling holiness. Jesus asked him to love him more than everything he had and come to understand what love is and whether Jesus, being the Christ, can do that.

Large parts of our beliefs are centered on what we have and are. Just as everything was taken from JOB, the only thing he had left was his beliefs, which Satan targeted.

Once you lose everything, you are left with your beliefs. A majority of your beliefs become unimportant at that point. A person will see past the ridiculous nature of a multitude of unneeded beliefs. Then losing yourself comes into play because beliefs are at the core of who we are.

Once you lose yourself completely you will find truth in God. John 8:31 says, "To the Jews who had believed him, Jesus said, *"If you hold to my teaching, you are really my disciples. Then you will know the truth, and the truth will set you free."*

The rich young ruler held on to the belief he had the whole picture, but Jesus told him he had part. The ruler had to add one thing to his beliefs. In order to do that, he had to understand being prosperous equated to nothing compared to believing Jesus was the Christ and following him. Jesus did not condemn him for being prosperous, only asked him to change his beliefs.

Jesus was offering the rich young ruler freedom. What Jesus was saying to the ruler was, "I want you in my service. I want you to do greater things. I want you to believe that I am God. I want you to be free." Jesus was offering life and the rich young ruler believed he already attained it because of his adherence to the law. Laws are there to help us have a great life, learn righteousness, but they will never help us see God, a savior, or anything else spiritual. Jesus challenged him to the core.

The rich young ruler went away sad because he, like others, had been waiting for the Christ to come and he was forced to choose whether Jesus was a prophet or the Christ because of Jesus' words. The ruler may or may not have heard Jesus' claims of being God in the flesh, but he knew something of Jesus to ask him the question he did.

The ruler certainly wanted to be validated by Jesus about the life he was living. He opened himself up to believe Jesus' words, but did not plan on the response Jesus gave him to get rid of everything he had and believe Jesus was the one to come, the Christ. He was sad because he away believed Jesus was a prophet, not the Christ, and not the way to eternal life. His choice was made on the very issue that made him wealthy in the first place, his obedience to the law and the evidence of being in God's favor by his wealth. Selling everything he had was opposite to everything he had learned from Jeremiah 29:11 where God wants to prosper us. Jesus answered and challenged the ruler's belief of who Jesus was and offered freedom at a price.

We all have a price for freedom. Some of us like me had several prices to pay and it was not cheap. I had to come to a belief I was not who I thought I was and come to a belief I was someone else, a child of God. I had to believe in God's view of me, which is completely different from my view of who I was. Luckily, I had not acquired riches God's way that would stop me from attaining this new view of who I was.

Jesus told the rich young ruler that God viewed him differently than he viewed himself. The rich young ruler did not accept it and went away sad because of his pride of who he had become using God's laws to do so. Being someone different in God's eyes must have sounded ridiculous to the rich young ruler at the time. Everything pointed to the young ruler as being right about his actions to be in accordance with God's laws. His beliefs were only partially right as Jesus pointed out.

Jesus' answer to the rich young ruler was similar to God's response to JOB's friends. God, at the end of the book, did not say JOB's friends were wrong in their thinking, only that they needed to offer a sacrifice. Jesus did not say the young ruler was wrong, only that he needed to offer a sacrifice. That sacrifice was his belief Jesus was the Christ and not only a prophet.

I am sure, because of the knowledge the ruler had, if he had given up his riches, he would have gotten them back because that is who he is as a person; that is if God had not planned to use him in a different way.

So, riches are preached about in church as an evil concept. Yes, they can be a snare where a person can rely on riches to take care of their needs and not allowing God to do so. King David was rich, King Saul was rich, and one made it to heaven and the other did not. If people do not get wealthy, how would the wealthy have a chance to hear about Jesus? The evil is not money itself but the beliefs surrounding money. The belief that God is more important than money is most important.

One of the most eye opening books I have ever read is God @ Work by Rick Marshall. I would try to say something about the book here but would not do it justice. I would implore you to read the book and come to an understanding, which is making its way into churches now.

We cannot fear having money or wealth in our life. God tells us not to fear anything except him, which leads to wisdom and love. You say, "How can I fear and love God at the same time." I say your life depends upon it.

What is your belief? Wealth does not get us to heaven. Righteousness alone does not get us to heaven. Love alone does not get us to heaven. Jesus was calling the rich young ruler to have the law and to believe he is the Christ. Jesus loved him by challenging his beliefs. God challenges our beliefs too. Be ready with your lamps lit, waiting for the day of change.

The Call

Aren't we confused most of the time about life? What is God doing in our life? Why is our life turning out the way it is or has? JOB had questions too because life was confusing at his time of testing. We will all go though something that challenges and tests our character. What will be your decision during those times; to remain righteous or unrighteous? What about your beliefs and holding on to who Jesus is?

The Pharisees, who practiced righteousness, many did not include love. The New Testament describes love and what it means to love another person. Righteousness and love, together, create a godly and holy character. Love without righteousness is futile. Make no mistake when Jesus says you must have righteousness beyond that of the Pharisees.

If you do NOT desire to be righteous at all costs, are you really trying to be like Jesus and JOB? Didn't Jesus make the right decision that saved your life? Aren't we supposed to be like Jesus and do the same, make righteous decisions at a cost of death, if necessary?

One thought I want you to throw around inside your head. Will God bless unrighteousness? I believe not. God can only bless you in your desire to be righteous. If you choose not to be righteous, God cannot bless you. Why would you be blessed for your unrighteousness?

Over and over again, God has blessed our desire to be righteous. I have never experienced God blessing me for my unrighteousness. The beauty is Jesus forgives us when we cannot be righteous and gives us a second chance to learn.

The call is to be righteous through the love of Jesus. We cannot focus only on love and expect to make it to heaven. We must make choices to be righteous at all costs.

Others must know our unrighteousness to help us strive to be righteous.

Unfortunately, righteousness and love have been separated in many churches to the dismay of God. Calling people to righteousness takes accountability though. We as people will get away with what we can if no one knows we are doing it. Our belief without accountability becomes, "I am okay because I love God and he loves me. I have confessed my sin to God." Commitment to being righteous and faithful is why JOB was recognized by God not because JOB loved God and people.

Let us think for a moment. Who would you want to be in heaven with? Someone who loves and sacrifices for others but smokes, gets drunk, and curses without a thought of making right decisions? Isn't trusting someone who is righteous and loving a much better combination?

Love is the doorway and the glue that holds each other part of godliness together. Many of us only want to do those portions of the Bible that are easy. Focusing only on loving is one of the easiest because we can sacrifice and serve far easier than making righteous decisions in the time of testing. Many become devoid of realizing the need to practice the rest of the Bible that says we must be righteous, obedient, faithful, and hopeful.

One of the coolest Latin sayings I have come across is Cor Ne Adito, which means, "Don't rip your heart." God is the one who tries to cure our hearts, but he gives us freedom of choice and freewill. Jeremiah 17:9 says, *"The heart is deceitful above all things and beyond cure. Who can understand it?"* Our deceit will rip our heart out and is the reason why continuing on the path to being righteous and loving is good for our heart. Some of our beliefs need to be changed to do so.

Your beliefs come from somewhere and are usually from your past, friends, or your preacher or pastor. Our beliefs are the foundation for our heart and mind. If we believe we can sin and still love God, we are deceived. Our beliefs about righteousness become blinded.

Who are you letting change your beliefs? Have you tested your preacher's spirit against what the Bible says or just "believe" he or she is saying the truth because of their position? If you are not digging into the Bible yourself, you will be prone to mis-beliefs by everyone around you.

Your beliefs are the strongest aspect of your character. Your beliefs are the foundation for everything you think, believe, and act upon. The importance of knowing what God wants you to believe compared to what people want you to believe will help you become aware of what beliefs are good for you and what beliefs are not.

Desiring NOT to understand your beliefs will lead a person to being swayed by the wind being tossed back and forth. Being overly confident of your beliefs is also a trap because a person becomes closed minded to anything that challenges his or her beliefs. We do not want Cor Ne Adito for our hearts or lives.

Our beliefs are being constantly challenged by the world around us including those of church. One of the most caustic beliefs instilled in Christians is that if you follow God, God will protect you.

Everyone one of us wishes for a hedge around our lives to keep us safe from Satan. We wish for a hedge that is impermeable, unbreakable, and guarded by angels. This belief that God will protect us at every turn is shattered when bad things happen to us. We start to come to a belief, "Does God not love me? Does God care for me still? If he did, wouldn't he protect me?" Our understanding waivers and at times destroys our lives. We walk away from God because we have changed our belief to "God does not care or God is absent."

If challenges were absent, how would our character of righteousness get stronger, our beliefs changed, faith deepen, and love become more complete? If we did not go through anything that pushes us to the point of making a right or wrong decision, how would God know we are worthy to be considered as JOB was considered? Many times, making the right decision causes us to rely completely on God supporting us through our situation. Relying on God, who we cannot see, will increase our faith. We need challenges for our growth.

I had a friend who was asked to lie about her job so the owners could get past an inquiry by the government. My friend decided not to lie about her job and she quit. Her character was challenged. She made the right decision but ended up having to leave. God was allowing the situation to unfold to see if she would make the right or wrong decision, and because she made the right decision, God blessed my friend afterward. If she had lied, she would still be at the same job with the guilt of the lie. She told the truth and was forced to open her own business, which in the end turned out for her prosperity. She will also have a deeper reliance on God to provide.

I have had my beliefs changed many times in my life. One of the most difficult beliefs to change was the belief I was in a one-of-a-kind church where every person was completely committed to God. Our church was growing at a rapid pace and practices were in place to train people to seek and save the lost. The statistics showed that for every three people committing to God, one person would walk away. It was very challenging to stay wholehearted and to give up every belief I had created throughout my lifetime while not being a disciple of Jesus. I needed to know everyone in church was completely committing to God at all costs because it helped me to do the same.

Coming from the world of sin into a relationship with God, a person needs to know they are in the right place among others who are also seeking God with all their heart in righteousness and love. Instilling the belief of being in a very unique or one true church of disciples was important to get my heart to give up every aspect of the world to be with God especially since I had seen so much hypocrisy in churches.

However, years later I realized there were people in other churches trying to do the same. I also opened up to "inconceivable events" such as demon possession. One event difficult to believe was watching people pray over someone who was believed to have a demon and then to see the difference in that person after the hours of prayer.

I realized through studying the Bible I had put the power of God into a box through the beliefs that were injected into me. I have to say, I started out on milk and then moved to solid food, so it was necessary to have those beliefs in the beginning, but then through growing in the knowledge of God, I allowed God himself to change my beliefs to where they needed to be.

I have learned every church has something they need to work on and no church is perfect. Each church has been put together by God to meet the needs of those people. I do believe some are doing better at it than others though.

We also have come to believe testing by God is tempting by Satan. God said "test" JOB not "tempt" him. I think of testing as I would a tomato and that means poking a tomato to see if it is ripe, if not, put it in a bag to ripen. Testing is not to hurt us, but to see how we are ripening and then to change the lighting or temperature to help us achieve God's ripeness for our lives. However, testing and tempting are a way to see whether we will make a right decision or not. I do not know anyone like JOB, but we should become like JOB in his righteousness.

My beliefs were challenged about writing a book. I always wanted to write children's books, but never got around to it mainly because I did not consider myself an adequate writer to do so. God had a different belief for me to grab onto and a much larger vision than I had. But then again, my ideas are not God's ideas many times.

Paul, an incredible man of God, was thrown into prison for a time. If Paul had not been thrown into prison, we would not have the letters we have today to read and apply to our lives. God had to throw Paul into prison to get him to write. Otherwise, Paul would have been out helping people become Christians, helping people remain Christians, helping the poor, and so on.

While in prison, Paul wrote the words from God we need to hear today in order to understand God's expectations and love. These letters were infused with joy, compassion, love, and peace while cooped up in a jail cell. How could someone write under such circumstances? How did Paul remain righteous during those times? God needed the rest of us to see, read, and understand the knowledge held within those words Paul wrote. God certainly does not do things the way we think things ought to be done.

While working at a job, I was given a vision to write a book. I kept telling myself I should write the book. God made sure I was given the time to write the book. I was fired from my job, could not find work, and did not even get a response from any company I sent resumes to for four months; all so I would finally conclude to write this book. This was not my idea of the best way to do things. I figured I would take time at night to write, which was an hour or two, in order to finish the book. God thought different and I am grateful for the experience.

My journey with this book has opened my eyes to many things in my life. I have learned a lot and changed my own beliefs through the process. My heart found a peace while writing I did not expect. I also came to some conflicting concepts about righteousness I do not have an answer.

Jesus says we must love one another including our enemies. We must be more righteous than the Pharisees. Together they complete us as individuals traveling the path to eternity. In opposition to loving your enemies, I will talk about a concept that is confusing to say the least and heart wrenching.

In the Sudan, Africa, the LRA, in opposition to the government, kills parents and abducts the children to turn them into fighters for their cause. These children are also used for other inhumane acts I will not talk about.

Sam Childers has made it his life work to help save those children from being abducted and brutally harmed. He goes out, rescues children being transported to the enemy camp by killing those driving the vehicles, and rescuing the children. Sam Childers claims to be Christian. Therein lies the conflict. Sam is rescuing children but killing people in the process. It is the right thing to do, don't you agree? I mean, if your child was being abducted, would you care how they were rescued? But yet, Jesus says pray for your enemies.

If all we did were pray, would the children be saved? Sam Childers loves those children, but if that was all he did was express his love for them, would that benefit them? He is making the right decision to act upon the atrocities. How about you? If all you do is love, but make no decision to act, what good is it? Shouldn't we make righteous decisions in our life to fight against evil? Isn't unrighteousness evil? JOB did.

John Eldridge wrote a book called Beautiful Outlaw. In the book, he mentions Jesus having fierce intentions as a character trait when confronting people and issues. Thinking further about this concept, I realized that Jesus had fierce intentions when he came to save us from being abducted by Satan. Jesus conquered death by his fierce actions in the garden and on the cross because of his love for us.

Sam Childers situation is a struggle in my heart. On one side, his is making the right decision to save the children, and the other side of me recognizes he is not making the right decision. The people in the LRA abducting the children were probably abducted children themselves.

A few scriptures that come to mind for the confusion that helps me a little. Genesis 4:6, God asks Cain, *"why is your face downcast? If you do what is right, will you not be accepted? But if you do not do what is right, sin is crouching at your door..."* God is saying if we do what is right, we will be accepted. If we do not do right, sin is at our door.

Numbers 25:7-8 points out that Phinehas ran a spear through the unrighteous Israelite man and woman and the plague was ended against Israel. God stated Phinehas turned his anger away from the Israelites *"...since he was zealous for my honor."* God thereafter made a covenant of peace with Phinehas and his descendants.

Is this what Sam Childers is doing? Are there different levels of righteousness? Are all the levels in between acceptable to God in the fight against unrighteousness? I find this challenging, to say the least, when I think about this concept.

So, I hope this book has opened your eyes a little and changed your beliefs. We are all facing death with a hope in God. Let us not be deceived and believe love is all you need, but a combination of love and righteousness. "Only loving" is not the answer, but part of the whole God expects.

Romans 8:3-4 says, *"For what the law was powerless to do because it was weakened by the flesh, God did by sending his own Son in the likeness of sinful flesh to be a sin offering. And so he condemned sin in the flesh, in order that the* **righteous requirement** *of the law might be fully met in us,* *who do not live according to the flesh but according to the Spirit.*" Jesus came so our flesh, which is weak, could be stronger in order to meet the "righteous requirement of the law." Jesus gives us the power to be righteous. Use it!

Being righteous is our choice, not God's. God provides the tools for our righteousness. We need to take those tools and use them to our benefit and that being eternity. It is only too late if we have died already, in which case you would not be reading this book. You have a chance now to change. You have the power to be the fulfillment of the law and prophets through the love of Jesus because Jesus was the fulfillment. Today is the day of salvation because tomorrow is not guaranteed, that is unless you live today as you should live in eternity, in righteousness and love. What do you believe?

I will close out this book with a speech by Samuel before he was taken into heaven.

Samuel's Farewell Speech

1st Samuel 12:2
I have been your leader from my youth until this day. 3 Here I stand. Testify against me in the presence of the Lord and his anointed. Whose ox have I taken? Whose donkey have I taken? Whom have I cheated? Whom have I oppressed? From whose hand have I accepted a bribe to make me shut my eyes? If I have done any of these things, I will make it right.

www.ingramcontent.com/pod-product-compliance
Lightning Source LLC
Chambersburg PA
CBHW071458070426
42452CB00041B/1913